WOLF GIRLS AT VASSAR

WOLF GIRLS
AT VASSAR

LESBIAN & GAY

EXPERIENCES

1930 – 1990

COMPILED AND EDITED BY

ANNE MacKAY

ST. MARTIN'S PRESS   NEW YORK

WOLF GIRLS AT VASSAR: LESBIAN AND GAY EXPERIENCES
1930–1990. Copyright © 1992, 1993 by Anne
MacKay. Foreword copyright © 1993 by Lillian
Faderman. All rights reserved. Printed in the United
States of America. No part of this book may be used
or reproduced in any manner whatsoever without
written permission except in the case of brief
quotations embodied in critical articles or reviews.
For information, address St. Martin's Press,
175 Fifth Avenue, New York, N.Y. 10010.

Frontispiece photo © Marianne Buchenhorner.

DESIGN BY JUDITH A. STAGNITTO

Library of Congress Cataloging-in-Publication Data

Wolf girls at Vassar : lesbian and gay experiences,
    1930–1990 / edited by Anne MacKay ;
foreword by Lillian Faderman.
        p. cm.
    ISBN 0-312-08923-6
    1. Lesbians—United States.   2. Gay men—
United States.   3. Vassar College—Alumni.
I. MacKay, Anne.
HQ75.6.U5W643   1993
3055.9'0664—dc20   92-42022
                                        CIP

First published by Ten Percent Publishing

First Revised Paperback Edition: June 1993

10   9   8   7   6   5   4   3   2   1

for Cynthia, Sylvia, and Freddie

and for

"The Lesbian Herstory Archives
Where our truths are cherished,
Our words preserved from
The burial of silence."

—*Adrienne Rich*

CONTENTS

ACKNOWLEDGMENTS

A great many people have helped in the preparation of this book. I would particularly like to thank Manuela Soares and Sara Yager for saying it was possible and making it a reality.

The following people from Vassar have been extremely kind and helpful: Nancy S. MacKechnie and Melissa J. O'Donnell of the Vassar Library Special Collections, Mary Gesek, Dixie Sheridan, Sherry Smith, and Georgette Weir.

Special thanks go to Cynthia Beer, Cristina Biaggi, Mary Barlow, Ardis Cameron, Betsy Crowell, Anne Cummings, Nancy Dean, Mary Dorman, Beva Eastman, Elizabeth A. Garfield, Lee Hudson, Nancy MacKay, Sylvia Newman, Emily-Sue Sloane, Janet Swanson, and Freddie Wachsberger.

I gratefully acknowledge permission to reprint the following:
Photograph of the Wolf Girls by Marianne Buchenhorner.
Excerpts from "My Coming Out Story" by Lisa Malachowsky.
"Breaking the Silence." *Vassar Quarterly*.
Drawings from *Everything Correlates*, by Jean Anderson.
"Madboy's Song" and "Song," by Muriel Rukeyser, by permission of William L. Rukeyser.
A special thanks to the Special Collections of the Vassar Library for permission to reprint several photographs from their collection.

The archival photos from 1870–1950 are intended only to illustrate the good times that women had together at a women's college, and should not in any way imply that the women pictured were homosexual. As one graduate from the 1960s said, the wonderful thing about a women's college was that you had to do everything on your own—if you didn't have a man for a play, *you* had to play that part yourself.

FOREWORD

BY LILLIAN FADERMAN

The writer of an article entitled "A New Women's College" that appeared in *Scribner's Monthly* in 1873 was less than enthusiastic at the prospect of the establishment of yet another institution of higher learning for females: "It is not necessary to go into particulars," he wrote, but "such a system [colleges for women] is unsafe." Why? He was somewhat coy in his explanation, but he clearly felt compelled to alert a naive public about the dangers inherent in a long-term congregation of bright, independent young women without the benefit of male company:

> The facts which substantiate this opinion would fill the public mind with horror if they were publicly known. Men may "pooh! pooh!" these facts if they choose, but they exist. Diseases of body, diseases of imagination, vices of body and imagination—everything we would save our children from—are bred in these great institutions where life and associations are circumscribed, as weeds are forced in hotbeds.*

But his description (whose tone seems borrowed from mid-nineteenth-century French novels and verse such as Balzac's *The Girl with the Golden Eyes* and Baudelaire's *The Flowers of Evil*, that were intrigued with lesbian exoticism and evil) had little meaning for Americans. In this country, love between women was still often described by the innocent term "romantic friendship."

However, there was more than a glimmer of truth in his suggestion that women's colleges were a "hotbed" of passionate female-female relationships. The young women who were pioneers in higher education for females had every reason to fall in love with

---

*"A New Women's College," *Scribner's Monthly* (Oct. 1873), 6: 748–49.

each other. They came to college from a culture that encouraged romantic friendship between unmarried women because it permitted them to exercise sensibility (a valued feminine attribute) while ostensibly preserving their virginity for marriage. The popular American writer Henry Wadsworth Longfellow described romantic friendship in his 1849 novel *Kavanagh* as "a rehearsal in girlhood for the great drama of woman's life." In a society where middle-class females generally had no hope of supporting themselves, such a "rehearsal" could not be threatening to the social fabric since women would have to marry—for economic reasons if no other.

Their society's general tolerance of romantic friendship between women and the fact that such relationships were not yet widely stigmatized as "lesbian" gave these pioneering college women permission to fall in love with each other. But their love was further encouraged by the heady fact of their being pioneers together, creating for the first time in American middle-class history a female peer culture unfettered by patriarchal dictates. They became heroes and leaders to one another, unhampered by male measuring sticks that might define, detract, or distract. The early women's colleges created a healthy and productive separatism such as radical lesbian-feminists of the 1970s might have envied. As Anne MacKay points out in her introduction to *Wolf Girls at Vassar*, "To be independent, to be able to learn all the things men learned, to create an all-absorbing female culture made for exciting times." These early college women's excitement about their situation often translated into an excitement about each other. Even the very Victorian Alfred Lord Tennyson had to acknowledge the erotics of such a situation, much as he loathed it: In his poem "The Princess," which essentially laughs at education for women, he describes female learning mates as "two women faster welded in one love/ Than pairs of wedlock." It is no wonder that numerous terms—"crushes," "smashes," "spoons," "raves"—soon needed to be coined to describe college women's passions for each other.

Young college women had excellent, mature models for their female same-sex passions. In most colleges women professors were not permitted to remain on the faculty if they married a man, though it is doubtful that many of them who possessed a real taste for erudition and the defiant spirit it took to become a woman of learning in their era would have chosen nineteenth-century heterosexual marriage with its endless domestic burdens. But these early women professors were drawn to each other not *faute de mieux*. They were supports for each other in a world that was still ambivalent about the notion of a learned woman. (Popular writers of the period often warned that an unprecedented variety of illnesses would be visited upon these new learned females who were forcing their brains to use up the blood they needed for menstruation.*) Like their students, women faculty members sparked on the excitement of being pioneers and kindred spirits together.

The female twosome was an accepted institution on the faculties of women's colleges in America in the late-nineteenth and early-twentieth century. Mount Holyoke's president from 1901 to 1937, Mary Woolley, lived during all that time with her "devoted companion," Jeannette Marks, head of the English Department. Bryn Mawr's first woman president, M. Carey Thomas, lived on campus with another English professor, Mamie Gwinn. Famous Wellesley College pairs included novelists Florence Converse and Vida Scudder, as well as composers of "America, the Beautiful," Katherine Lee Bates and Katherine Coman. Their lives as faculty couples were openly played out on campus. Love between women in the early decades of the women's college was a noble tradition.

It continued to be a noble tradition well into the twentieth century. In her autobiographical 1928 novel about Vassar, *We Sing Diana*, Wanda Fraiken Neff, who had been both a student and a professor there, recalls an Eden of female-female love at the time her character becomes a freshman, in 1913. Romance between women on that campus was considered "the great human experience." Violent crushes on a particular woman professor had run to such epidemic proportions that she was called "The Freshman Disease." But in the 1920s, when the heroine comes back to campus to teach, all has changed. The country has just been through the Great War, which, ironically, promoted feminist progress, opening jobs to many more women and finally helping them gain the vote because of their contributions to the war effort. Feminist successes

---

*See, e.g., Edward H. Clarke, *Sex in Education, or, A Fair Chance for Girls* (Boston: J. R. Osgood, 1873) and A. Hughes Bennett, "Hygiene in the Higher Education of Women," *Popular Science Monthly*, Feb. 1888.

meant that society was forced to take women more seriously as adult human beings, and female-female passionate relationships could no longer be dismissed as "a rehearsal in girlhood for the great drama of woman's life." If large numbers of women were now potentially independent beings, what was to stop them from making that "rehearsal" the "great drama" itself?

In addition, knowledge, or pseudoknowledge, of "sexual abnormality" through the popularization of the writings of sexologists, most notably Sigmund Freud, meant that the innocence implicit in the phrase used to describe love between women, "romantic friendship," was subject to scrutiny as it had not been earlier. Neff reflects that scrutiny in her novel. By the 1920s at Vassar, undergraduate speech is full of Freudian vocabulary; everything is attributed to sex; and "intimacies between two girls were watched with keen, distrustful eyes. Among one's classmates, one looked for the bisexual type, the masculine girl searching for a feminine counterpart, and one ridiculed their devotions."

Not all college students shared the jaded suspicions of Vassar women in the 1920s. The Bryn Mawr yearbook for 1921 contains a senior essay, "My Heart Leaps Up," that affectionately reflects the still-ubiquitous nature of female love in academia in those years during and just after the Great War:

> Crushes are bad and happen only to the very young and very foolish. Once upon a time we were very young, and the bushes on campus were hung with our bleeding hearts. Cecil's heart bled indiscriminately. The rest of us specialized more, and the paths of Gertie Hearne, Dosia, Eleanor Marquand, Adelaide, Tip and others would have been strewn with roses if public opinion had permitted flowers during the War. . . . The real thing in the way of passion was the aura of emotion with which Kash surrounded Sacred Toes. She confided her feelings to one-half the campus, and the other half was not in total ignorance, but Kash constantly worried lest it should leak out.*

Such innocence about the stigma surrounding homosexuality was also suggested by the Oberlin College yearbook for 1920 which contains a page of thirty-two photographs of young women who

---

*Bryn Mawr College yearbook, 1921, quoted in Catharine R. Stimpson, "The Mind, the Body, and Gertrude Stein," *Critical Inquiry* (1977), 3: 491–506.

are identified by name under the heading "Lesbians." They were members of the Oberlin Lesbian Society, a women's group devoted to writing poetry.*

But by the 1930s, the changes in attitudes and perceptions with regard to love between women had invaded all American colleges. As Anne MacKay observes in her introduction, "But now, if you were aware you loved women, you knew you were in trouble." MacKay's wonderful collection of memories by lesbians and (beginning in the 1970s) gay men at Vassar reveals how they dealt with that "trouble" and how they eventually succeeded in turning Vassar around to make same-sex love as safe on that campus as it had been during the earlier years when women's college campuses were a haven for women who loved women.

Anne MacKay's request in the *Vassar Quarterly* in 1989 to lesbian and gay alumni for stories about their Vassar experiences brought her dozens of varied responses—a woman who was a student in the 1930s and remembers that she was so petrified someone would find out she was a lesbian that she "wound up in the infirmary every once in a while at the edge of some kind of breakdown"; another lesbian student in the 1950s who was sent by the dean to "the school shrink who told me I was evil . . . and I was asked to leave school"; a young man who entered in 1970 with the first freshman class to include males and who "projected a consciously and openly gay persona," the effect of which was to get him elected class president during his freshman, sophomore, and senior years; a woman student of the class of 1990 who found at Vassar a "wonderfully supportive, intellectually exciting and strongly affirming" community in which to come out as a lesbian.

Their tales and many others are told in Vassar alumnae/i's own voices in this valuable record of lesbian and gay academic life. These stories that Anne MacKay has gathered also give us broader historical insights: They demonstrate the extent to which the social climate has the power to define us as "sickos" or as "leaders," though we and the meaning of our love have not changed. They reveal as well our efforts as lesbians and gay men to define ourselves, both in times of adversity and in times of societal support. They are moving testimonies to our struggles and our victories.

*Oberlin College yearbook pictures in New York Lesbian Herstory Archives, file: History, 1920s.

"Gail got these two wolf skins from her father,
so we decided to wear them—tied over
the shoulder, like Hercules—everyone else
was wearing Bermuda shorts—and we went out
and howled. We howled in the morning
and we howled at night."

CRISTINA BIAGGI '59

"I wanted to go to Vassar because of
the good choir and the good Drama Department,
but what really clinched it was when I went for
my interview and some friends told me about
the Wolf Girl—somebody who put on a wolf
skin and went howling around the Circle
in the full moon. That's me, I thought.
There's room for me!"

LUCY CROSS '61

WOLF GIRLS
AT VASSAR

INTRODUCTION

THE GIFT TO BE FREE

'Tis the gift to be simple, 'tis the gift to be free
'Tis the gift to come down where we ought to be.
When we find ourselves in the place just right
'Twill be in the valley of love and delight.

—TRADITIONAL SHAKER SONG

In 1970 I was feeling heady with the winds of women's and gay liberation. I approached Vassar, the college I had loved so much, with the hope of sharing ideas and experiences with alumnae and beginning a dialogue about the gay experience at Vassar and in America. The response from the *Vassar Alumnae Magazine* was a curt refusal (see Appendix A: "Being Gay at Vassar").

So it was with delight that in 1989, I accepted an invitation from the Alumnae & Alumni of Vassar College (AAVC) Ad Hoc Committee to speak, first to them and then to the entire Council, as an openly gay Vassar alumna. AAVC was then exploring the notion of including a gay "affinity group" in its organization. Unsure about the outcome of their investigation, Eric Marcus '80 took steps to found a gay organization, Lesbian and Gay Alumnae/i of Vassar College (LAGA/VC), and I put in a request in the *Vassar Quarterly* for stories of lesbian and gay experiences at Vassar, to start to reach out to alumnae/i. In 1990 the *Quarterly* printed my article "Breaking the Silence" (see Appendix B). This book, *Wolf Girls at Vassar*, contains the replies I received to that request and the article.

One major theme that runs through the book is how young people deal with a fact about themselves which they didn't ask for and which is still disagreeable to society. Some embraced their difference early in life yet fell back on avoidance and denial when faced with the censure of family and peers. Even today, parents are still reading mail and going through wastebaskets to discover what they consider to be the horrid facts about their children. In 1986, during spring break, one father had gone into his daughter's room and read her journal. Her lover recalls, "He had beaten her severely and fractured her jaw, which was why it was so hard for her to talk, and said he was going to kill her. Then he took her out of Vassar." In a recent case, some love letters were discovered. The parents told their daughter she "was sick, perverted, and that Vassar had corrupted her. After all, they raised her to be a good Christian. Why did she have to treat them this way?" Another mother threatened, "If I ever find out both my daughters are gay, I'll kill myself."

For many young Vassar women (and later, men), the loneliness and pain were unbearable. Psychiatrists were often brought in for a "cure," but they, along with most other professionals, often merely succeeded in intensifying pain and self-loathing. Vassar's administration was not kind to young women whose only crime was to have fallen in love. (It should be noted that harsh punishments also fell on any woman who became pregnant or defied the college rules about alcohol, men, and absence from dormitories.) In the last decades, however, the Vassar administration has been supportive of gay students, who are now the victims of harassment mostly from their male peers.

Another theme running through these writings is the very long time it has taken many women to discover that they were lesbians. Some found out at college, others later in life. Many came to Vassar intending to find the "right" boyfriend. Then one day: ". . . she stares at me and calmly says 'not until you kiss me.' So here I am being propositioned by my closest friend—the girl I spend time talking about boys with—and I kiss her. I'll never forget that kiss, and I know she won't either."

In spite of the misery many women experienced, the tributes to Vassar are stunning. They speak of the beauty of the campus, the excellent curriculum and faculty. "All around us were impressive, strong, feisty, smart, and very respectable women who had made it on their own." "Vassar, led by remarkable women in crucial positions of power, had presented models of distinguished achievements to its undergraduates." "There couldn't have been a better time or place for my coming out during my four years at Vassar."

As homosexuals we live outside an important part of our culture and are doubly aware of the tremendous system at work to make one become heterosexual. It starts the day we are born and continues relentlessly. I can remember in first grade being forced to choose a boy to give a present to. Every year the messages became stronger—about clothes, looks, being submissive, not being too smart, being on "good" behavior, not being a tomboy or a wolf girl, not encroaching on male territory—carpentry, science, cars, and so forth. For the women in these accounts, a feminist perspective has become a sustaining force and a necessity.

This collection is for all who continue to face the struggle to be themselves. It is also for our classmates who may find that their children are gay, and for all our other classmates who lived down the hall or sat next to us in English 105—good friends we comforted when they went through bad times but with whom we rarely could share why we were miserable.

While the stories here offer a variety of experiences, they come from only a tiny fraction of Vassar graduates who are homosexual. Not included here are those who were unable to survive their own and society's scorn. Many entered into loveless yet respectable marriages, others suffered too much emotional or sexual damage or became alcohol and drug dependent.

The good news is that more and more of us are strong and resilient survivors. The graduates whose stories appear here are clear about wanting to be seen as people who have dared to be themselves. The struggle for "the gift to be free" was well worth it.

1 8 6 1 — 1 9 0 0   Vassar in its earliest years must have been heaven for women. To be independent, to be able to learn all the things men learned, to create an all-absorbing female culture made for exciting times. Helen Lefkowitz Horowitz in her book *Alma Mater* (Beacon Press, 1984) has a chapter called "Acting a Manly Part" in which she describes the incredibly complex and self-contained social life that sprang up at Vassar and other women's colleges. Teas, rituals, "spreads" (food parties, often at night), and all kinds of high jinks and fun absorbed almost every student—except the super-serious, called then, as now, "grinds." The 1866 college catalogue tells us that, "Some of the chambers contain single and others double beds, to suit the different tastes and circumstances of the students." Overcrowding (for financial reasons) soon meant that a great many students shared beds.* Corridor teachers could be evaded for midnight visits or sleepovers. Long skirts ("Young ladies are not supposed to have feet," said Miss Lyman, the Lady Principal[†]) were no impediment to hikes, baseball clubs, or adventures. Recent research has given Vassar the honor of the first female baseball team, called a "club" then, in 1866.[‡] I remember reading when I was at Vassar about some of the early students who were caught exploring the huge steam tunnels that run under the Quad. Philaletheis, the lovers of truth, started as a literary society and quickly became a dramatic group with three chapters and two-thirds of the student body as members. And everyone was free to love, and to express that love with notes, embraces, locks of hair, and kisses.

If you felt excessive admiration for someone, usually a beautiful or talented younger student, it was called a "smash." *The Cornell Times* in 1873 reprinted a letter written to the *Yale Courant* to explain this "term in general use at Vassar . . . 'smashing.' "[§]

---

*Helen Lefkowitz Horowitz. *Alma Mater*. Boston: Beacon Press, 1984, p. 39.

[†]Elaine Kendall. *Peculiar Institutions*. New York: G. P. Putnam's Sons, 1975, p. 107.

[‡]Special Collections, Vassar Library.

[§]Horowitz, op. cit., p. 67.

The "Resolutes," an early Vassar baseball club *(photo courtesy of the Vassar College Library)*

When a Vassar girl takes a shine to another, she straightaway enters upon a regular course of bouquet sendings, interspersed with tinted notes, mysterious packages of "Ridley's Mixed Candies," locks of hair perhaps, and many other tender tokens, until at last the object of her attention is captured, the two become inseparable, and the aggressor is considered by her circle of acquaintances as—"smashed." The mortality, so to

A fancy dress party in 1887 *(photo © Vail Bros., Poughkeepsie, NY; photo courtesy Vassar College Library)*
Pictured: Nellie Wooster '86, Mary Anderson '87, Gertrude Cleveland '87, Belle Skinner '87, Lucie F. Vance '87, Clara Blackwell '88, Rose Foster '88, Eliza McCreery '88, Frances Patterson '88, Louise Wooster '88, Alice Haliday '89, Delia Norris '89, Mary Dameron (Countess Reventlow-Criminil) Spec.

speak, resulting from these smashups, is frightful to contemplate. One young lady, the "irrepressible," rejoices in more than thirty. She keeps a list of them, in illuminated text, framed and hung up in her room like a Society poster. . . . Vassar numbers her smashes by the score.

One faculty member regarded the prevalence of smashing a "pest" and resented the time it took away from students' studies. If emotions got too out of hand, administrators were forced to provide different rooming arrangements. Horowitz makes the point that, from the start, administrators had worried that education would masculinize women's minds and attitudes, and it was these women's

HAVING FUN AT THE TURN OF THE CENTURY

Carline Sperry '02 and Jessie Miller '02 *(photo courtesy of the Vassar College Library)*

Helen English ex '04 and Bonner Semple '03 *(photo courtesy of the Vassar College Library)*

independence that threatened them, not any sexual implications. Loving friendships and passionate female attachments were common in the centuries before ours, and regarded as natural (see Lillian Faderman's excellent book, *Surpassing the Love of Men*, William Morrow, 1981). But the administrators really started to worry when it was announced in 1895 that out of 1,082 women Vassar had graduated, only 409 had married, and they were hard put to explain this startling fact to the world at large. The figures were similar for the other women's colleges.*

1900–1930   By the turn of the century, being "smashed" had been replaced by being "crushed." This time, it was usually the younger student who admired the older one and pursued her with flowers and gifts. Seniors or juniors could

*Kendall, op. cit., p. 127.

WARTIME ACTIVITIES—CA. 1918

Farmerette driving a tractor (*photo © Brown Bros., New York; photo courtesy of the Vassar College Library*)

respond to these attentions, but now were considered too grown up to initiate them. We have records of the wonderful student culture that flourished at that time, but little has been written about the women who loved women. The word "lesbian" had been coined but was not in current use. The "Boston marriage," in which two women lived together, was considered a sensible solution to the economic and social conditions Victorian and Edwardian women faced. Faculty members might live together in close relationships. After all, as we were constantly told, what women did, separately or together, wasn't really very important.

In high school, I was taught by and later became a colleague of a woman who grew up in this period. If she had grown up in recent years, she would have felt comfortable as a lesbian. She was tall, handsome, independent, an author and artist who had not been able to go to college and had little interest in marrying. Colleagues who were of a later generation than hers presumed that her 30-year loving relationship with another woman was a lesbian one, meaning that it was a sexual relationship. I think that it was *not* sexual, but feel that it was lesbian because when they described their first times together it seemed clear that they were in love. I once overheard a high school friend of hers (they were both then in their 80s) ask her, "And what happened to that *beautiful* girl you simply *snatched* away from England?" What happened was that at age 65, when she retired from teaching, the "beautiful girl" left the relationship and married an old friend, a widower, who had reappeared. Although there had been no stigma attached to long-term affectionate relationships in those early days, it was clearly understood that marriage was more desirable, and expected, if possible.

The reverse of this story was mentioned in "Breaking the Silence": a happily married woman who came out as a lesbian at age 70. The summer 1991 *Vassar Quarterly* class notes from 1926 tell us that the woman was a Vassar alumna: "Elizabeth (Buffy) T. Dennison tells us now that she has 19 grandchildren and 17 great-grandchildren . . . Buffy was amused by the article 'Breaking the Silence' in the recent *Quarterly*. 'The Boston woman described (in parenthesis) is me. The videotape is called *It's Never Too Late*—very true.'"

Edna St. Vincent Millay '17 *(left)* acting in the Vassar production of George Bernard Shaw's *Candida. (photo courtesy of the Vassar College Library)*

HAVING FUN IN THE TWENTIES

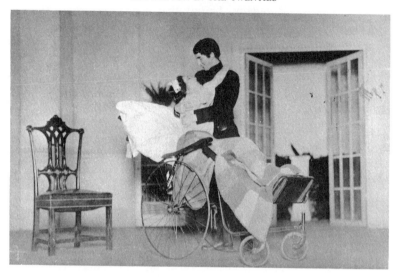

Two unidentified Vassar students in "A Kiss for Cinderella," 11 March 1922 *(photo © E. L. Wolven; photo courtesy of the Vassar College Library)*

One alumna we do know a little about was Edna St. Vincent Millay. She entered Vassar in 1913, four years older than her classmates, having been sponsored and given financial aid on the basis of her poetry. It was still a time when deep affections for women were common, but her feelings were so intense and effusive that her early biographer, Jean Gould in *The Poet and Her Book* (Dodd Mead & Company, 1969), seems embarrassed by them. "Vincent" became popular by acting in plays, being full of fun and wit, and exceptionally creative. Any lesbian who reads her poem "Interim," as I did in high school, instantly responds to the accuracy of the emotion, the beautiful, tremendously powerful moment when love is first expressed between two young women. Much of the poem unfortunately is not very good but does include some interesting lines, including "If only God had let us love—and show the world the way!" Information about her lesbianism and later bisexuality can be found in Lillian Faderman's book, *Odd Girls and Twilight Lovers* (Columbia University Press, 1991).

"We were in love with all things Greek." A spring celebration in the Shakespeare Garden. *(Undated photograph courtesy of the Vassar College Library)*

My mother went to Vassar in the mid-'20s, and I heard many stories of friendships and cocoa parties in her small select group. I was named for her best friend who remembered how "Your mother and I took constant long walks, saying poetry 'at' each other."

Once when I was about 14, and looking through Mother's Vassar yearbook, I asked her about a handsome woman, the head of their Athletic Association, but didn't get much of a reply. My mother's friend remembered this woman from their common school, Madeira, and said she had been asked to leave. "Looking back, I am sure she was gay, and would have thought so then if I had known the word." Their class notes a few years ago mentioned this woman's death in England, where she had lived with her companion of many years.

HAVING FUN IN THE THIRTIES

Four unidentified Vassar students in an unidentified dramatic production, ca. 1932 (*photo © E. L. Wolven; photo courtesy of the Vassar College Library*)

1 9 3 0 — 1 9 5 0   When I look back, the '30s and '40s seem to have been a time of innocence. Through the Depression and World War II, the "love that dares not speak its name" was very silent. A story was told in Raymond House when I was in my first year: two senior roommates came back from their comprehensive exams totally drained, fell down together on their living room couch, and passed out. A freshman on message center (no phones in those days!) came up with an urgent message, knocked, and when there was no answer, opened the door. Seeing them on the couch she said, "Oh, I'm *terribly* sorry—I didn't know you were busy!" This story was told with affection both for the innocent friendship of the seniors and the innocence of the freshman. The extraordinary cartoons by Anne Cleveland '36 and Jean Anderson '33, capture the charm and simplicity of this period at Vassar in *Everything Correlates* and *Vassar, a Second Glance*. They also illus-

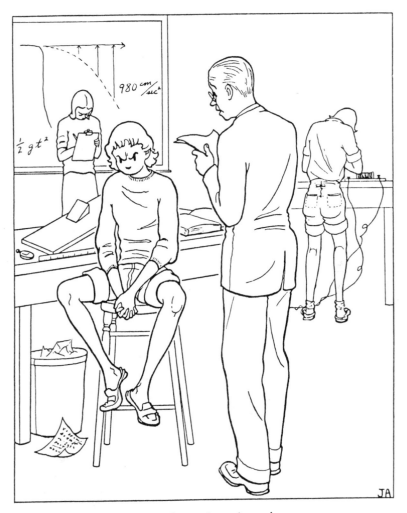

"But Miss Witherspoon, just what *is* there about the
law of gravity that you find yourself unable to accept?"

Drawing by Jean Anderson from *Everything Correlates*, "Some Observations
on the Educational Continuum," by Anne Cleveland and Jean Anderson

trate the beginnings of the blue jeans era and cut-off pants with large men's shirts over them—the first unisex clothing.

But now, if you were aware you loved women, you knew you were in trouble. Vassar's second major poet, Elizabeth Bishop '34, was a lesbian, and may have been the model for Lakey in *The Group* by Mary McCarthy '33. For those who never read this epic, Lakey turns up after college with a lesbian lover and becomes an important, strong character in the book. (For more information about Elizabeth Bishop's affairs, see "The Annals of Poetry—Elizabeth Bishop in Brazil," *The New Yorker*, September 30, 1991.) At the same time as Bishop, another poet, Muriel Rukeyser '34, was struggling with her feelings for women. The poem "Madboy's Song" is a heartbreaking testament to this conflict. When I was in high school, her poetry seemed special to me. In 1965 I directed her son in a play. Some years later I heard her speak to a lesbian group in Manhattan, and realized why she had seemed special. She said that being there was a "coming home" for her.

HAVING FUN IN THE FORTIES

Soph Party, Jan 31/Feb 1, 1947
Cover drawing: Bibs Muhs '48

Judy (Jeff) Williamson '48 & Bibs Muhs '48 sing "When I See Magnolias in Your Eyes"

Another graduate from this period was Elizabeth Moffatt Drouil-het '30, Vassar's warden (later called the dean of residence), known as "the Drou," who appears many times in these pages. When I was at college, she lived in the Warden's House by the Circle. I was there a lot because of student government affairs and remember being fascinated by the procession of close friends who would come to share the house with her.

The war years meant that social trips to men's colleges were restricted, as transportation and men were often lacking. For those who loved Vassar, the weekends were a wonderful time for all sorts of activities. It became the era of the great musicals; Soph Party and Junior Party were full shows with original scripts and music—and the songs were terrific. My Soph Party was a feminist dream: the heroine rejected the prince, the outdoors man, and the tough Bogart character, who were all pressuring her to become their property. She said she didn't want to be stereotyped, she wanted to be herself, and make her own decisions. Lesbianism of course was *not* a possible choice then. Any lesbian who found love during those years was very quiet about it. Most went through difficult times falling in love with friends who were either straight or could not acknowledge their feelings. Some ended up in the infirmary with illnesses or "breakdowns;" a few chose suicide. Kinsey's statistics said that 10 percent of the population was gay, even if they were not acting on it. If I had known about this in the 1940s, I would have guessed that barely one percent at Vassar was homosexual. What I have realized lately is how long it takes many women to come to a true understanding of their sexuality. Being attracted to your own sex was so unacceptable and frightening that most women could not move from attraction to a real lesbian love. The number of women is large who realized their preference for women later in life.

1950–1970 The years of "normalcy" and conformity after World War II brought social life back to Vassar with a vengeance—buses carried "boys" to Vassar and took "girls" away to men's colleges constantly. The togetherness of the last decades declined. When I was at Vassar we sang all the time, at dinner, after dinner, outdoors, anywhere. In the '50s there were still plays and activities and octets, but the singing and "bond-ing" faded away, the spirit had gone. One lesbian writes, "I arrived at Vassar and immediately experienced the feeling of 'being other.' " The word lesbian was used openly now and there were rumors of "lesbian rings" and lesbians who "danced nude under the moon." It was a repressive period in America and for lesbians at Vassar, a time of terror. "A witch hunt, albeit a quiet one, was whipping through the place." "Miss Blanding said that if I didn't relate the names of my friends to her (she had a legal pad handy) they would fix it so that I could not be accepted in any college or university in the U.S. ever."

Was there a systematic clearing out of lesbians at Vassar in the '50s? The students thought so, but one administrator from those days who is still alive says she could not believe such a thing. When I was a student, I had seen President Blanding be very compassion-ate to a student who I later knew to be a lesbian. Academic failure, heavy rule-breaking, and alcohol abuse were probably the causes of most expulsions. The college policy seems to have been that if a student was known to be a lesbian and was repentant (and not failing), she could remain at Vassar *if* she saw the school psychiatrist.

What we do know is that the college had come under fire in 1951 when Dr. Carl Binger, a psychiatrist, resigned as head of the Mellon foundation at Vassar (a grant given to study academic and personal advising of students). His assertion that Vassar was a matriarchy made front-page news in the *New York Times* and other papers. With patriarchy the undisputed norm, this was a shocking indictment. At that time matriarchy was not only a bad thing, but implied lesbianism. In case you missed his point, he went on to say, "I don't believe that matriarchy provides a wholesome atmosphere in which students are likely to develop satisfactorily." He said he was con-cerned about "sexual developments of undergraduates in an atmo-sphere of supervision by matriarchy" and there were "too many unmarried women at Vassar in supervisory capacities."* It was never mentioned, of course, that male colleges did very well without women. In those schools, females were rarely hired to teach, much less for supervisory roles. I like to think that all this was because Dr. Binger had come up against the warden, Elizabeth Drouilhet,

---

*quoted in the *Poughkeepsie New Yorker*, May 31, 1951.

Main Building hung with a banner for the LAGA/VC Conference, April 1991 (*photo © Anne MacKay*)

and lost. But whatever the cause, it was Vassar that was the loser; it was a heavy and low blow.

By 1960 plans were afoot to make Vassar more coeducational (read heterosexual). Merging and mating with Yale in New Haven was finally understood to be a form of suicide, so admitting men seemed the best solution to the diminishing enrollment all women's colleges were facing. When Miss Blanding retired, a man was chosen to be Vassar's new leader.

Outside of Vassar, change was in the air, and the Vietnam war was brewing revolution: student revolution, sexual revolution, black and women's liberation, and, finally, gay liberation. The Stonewall uprising took place in June 1969. Things would never be "normal" again, though it would take a while for the effects to reach Vassar.

1 9 7 0 — 1 9 9 0   In 1970 Carla Duke '73 posted a notice at Vassar for women to come and talk about feminism. Over 100 women showed up. After she and some friends participated in the N.O.W. conferences and invited Kate Millett and Rita Mae Brown to speak, "the net effect on the campus was a full-blown radical lesbian group of five to ten women, which seemed to have sprung from the forehead of Athena."

If Vassar had brought men in for a more "normal" atmosphere, the administration had forgotten that there would be gay men. Little did they know that Jackie Saint James (Remi St. Cloud) '74, a member of the first class to graduate men, would get full media coverage for his visible gay presence. It was a time for gay visibility to begin in all colleges, but soon the word was that Vassar would start heavy recruitment for rugby players. Anyone who has visited the college store has also seen the masculinization of the college colors; the beautiful rose and grey has given way to maroon and stronger shades.

Until the late 1960s, one's sexuality was usually explored with caution and often fear. Abortions had been illegal, expensive, and dangerous. Contraceptive devices were embarrassing to get. Sex was often not a positive experience, given the lack of knowledge on both sides. After the sexual revolution it became an imperative to explore one's sexuality: virginity meant you were missing out on all the good things that were being promoted with "turning on" to the sexual revolution (and drugs). For some lesbians, drinking had always provided an illusion of self-esteem and numbed the pain. Drugs would provide an even worse solution. The rules were changing rapidly on campus. One day the college insisted on knowing where you were every minute, the next day no one cared where you were, or who shared your room with you.

One powerful effect of the sexual revolution was to make homosexuality a viable choice for people. Many alumnae/i allowed themselves to leave marriages and lead openly homosexual lives. On campus, it was permissible to experiment, and the new gay organizations that formed gave support. Lesbian and gay communities began to develop. Unfortunately there are always people who would like to oppress others. One recent graduate writes:

> In the larger Vassar community I never felt any personal hostility though I had friends in both worlds. I saw hostility on

campus; signs being ripped down and graffiti. I saw horrible things being written in the bathrooms, but I remember the more violent comments being written on the library carrels: "Homosexuals should be shot," "Queers go home." There was one counselor at the Center who was incredibly insensitive about things he said to gay students. I heard lots of harassment stories about people being yelled at just walking down the paths. There was one Town House that had all lesbian and gay students, and people would drive by and scream out, "Fucking Dykes!" or "Fags!" I don't remember any acts of physical violence.

Toward the end of my time at Vassar there was a really good discourse that went on in the women's bathrooms—graffiti on one side from the straight women and graffiti from the lesbians on the other side, and often they would start talking to each other. There were some interesting exchanges. It seemed as if people were listening to each other!

I think that the survey from the task force, when it was circulated and the results posted, increased awareness about hostility. People took notice. Acts of harassment had never been documented before. Some well-liked and important faculty—straight and gay—were on the committee and that was a really important statement.

It is exciting now to see Vassar become part of the richness of the growing multicultural sensibility, and I hope that people who read these stories can take away some understanding of the diversity of the lesbian and gay experience—the pain of finding that you don't fit the usual pattern, the strength that comes from adversity, the struggle to preserve one's self, to be true to one's nature, the joy and delight of loving relationships. As Ann Northrop '70 says, "Until the world sees us wherever we are, whoever we are, whatever we are doing, in our full existence, we will not get as far as we need to go. I think that is the key: being visible."

It is always hard to know what the future will bring, but the strength of President Fergusson's leadership is impressive. She wrote in December 1990 (in reference to "Breaking the Silence"):

I have been very pleased by the positive response we have had for LAGA/VC. Indeed, I have received only happy letters from alumnae/i and not a single negative response. The world, at least at Vassar, does mature, thank goodness.

The delight that lesbian and gay alumnae/i felt at the April 1991 conference has lasted a long time. A postcard from an older alumna after the conference summed it up: "When my 17-year-old self and I walked our old path through the campus Saturday night, we were light with the gift of freedom."

—Anne MacKay '49
Orient, New York, 1991

Anne MacKay, 1949

Anne MacKay, 1991 *(photo © Raj John)*

MURIEL RUKEYSER

MADBOY'S SONG

Fly down, Death: Call me:
I have become a lost name.

One I loved, she put me away,
        Fly down, Death;
Myself renounced myself that day,
        Fly down, Death.
My eyes in whom she looked so deep
        Long ago flowed away,
My hands which slept on her asleep
        Withered away,
My living voice I meant to keep,
        Faded and gray.

Fly down, Death: Call me:
I have become a lost name.

Evening closes in whispers,
    Dark words buried in flame.
My love, my mother, my sister,
    I know there is no blame;

But you have your living voice,
    Speak my forgotten name.

Fly down, Death: Call me:
I have become a lost name.

Don't come for me in a car
To drive me through the town;
Don't rise up out of the water,
Once is enough to drown;
Only drop out of the sky,
For I am fallen down.

S O N G

The world is full of loss; bring,
    wind, my love.
My home is where we make our
    meeting-place,
And whatever I shall touch
    and read
Within that face.

Lift, wind, my exile from my eyes;
    Peace to look, life to listen and
        confess,
Freedom to find to find to find
That nakedness.

LENORE THOMPSON

*My Vassar years were hell. But
there wasn't much alternative to
pulling myself together and
struggling on silently.*

All my life, I was one of the silent minority. But I think I should speak out now, both to insist that my longings are part of the human range, and that a multitude of years need not bar one from fulfillment.

I graduated from Vassar in 1940—Dean's List—but in fact I just about made it through college without some kind of nervous breakdown or psychotic break, because I knew very well where things were at with me, and I was terrified. Afterward I took the path away from too much involvement with individual people, and became a college teacher, and later, wouldn't you know it, a psychotherapist. Along the way a young man who shared many of my interests (radical politics, camping) wanted to marry me. This seemed like a plausible solution to what otherwise didn't seem to have any solution at all. We had four children, and for a dozen years I was very busy being a mother. Forbidden feelings kept cropping up, but I kept my mind on motherhood, my job, community activities, conservation and camping, peace movement leadership, and my various avocations such as writing.

One day I discovered I was about to be 67. The knowledge that time was running out hit me. What was unfinished in my one chance at life? I knew there were two things; and I went to work at once to achieve them. One was to finish my autobiographical story (my posthumous statement to the world). The other was to achieve whatever I had missed in not acknowledging and experiencing the kind of love I had always dreamed of. I had heard of SAGE (Senior Action in a Gay Environment) through the women's movement, and one day I took the subway down there (terrified!) and started attending their rap groups. Soon I found there were also local lesbian groups. Fate was very gracious to me. Or perhaps, "When the pupil is ready, the teacher appears." Although I was now 68, I met a young woman who was not turned off by my age, and we became the lovers I had always dreamed of.

I should add that a dozen years of analysis were essential in freeing me from the demons that had strangled my past.

I am 72 now. Unfortunately, after four and a half years, my lover felt she had to return with her children to her husband's country when he was transferred back overseas; and I too felt I could not leave an aging husband who had been loyal to me (even knowing the situation).

I am still working, active, part of the local lesbian network. When I forget I am 72 (which is, in fact, most of the time), I wonder what I will find in the years ahead.

As for my experiences at Vassar, in 1936–40 gayness was the love that had no name. I felt passionately toward one of my class-mates, but I was petrified someone would find out, and wound up in the infirmary every once in a while at the edge of some kind of breakdown. My doctor said I "took life too seriously," which is doubtful. My Vassar years were hell. But there wasn't much alterna-tive to pulling myself together and struggling on silently. Ironically, I am sure my classmate was/is gay. Until I was 68, my gayness was my secret.

I am "out" at work now, and I no longer make any big secret of my feelings. It is my judgment that at this point in life no one can hurt me much, and I think I owe it to my sisters to be an example. It hasn't made any difference to my friends or co-workers. My children always knew I was a little off-center. It has mattered only to my husband, who didn't expect this kind of ending in the marriage.

NAME WITHHELD

To be with someone who loved you
was an incredible experience.

When I was 14, my sailing buddy (female) kissed me one night (just practice for her), and I thought I was going to fly away. I was sure that my family would see me when I came home and instantly know what had happened. While it didn't seem wrong at all, I knew this was not something to share with the world. I had always hated the word "crush." It seemed a putting down of the love I felt for friends or older students. These feelings for women were my private world, my secret life.

Although I had visited Vassar the year before, I had forgotten until I arrived that there would be *people* there, people my own age, all different and wonderful. Down the hall was another freshman who became an instant friend. That first week she seduced me emotionally, left love notes, and we even spent a close (non-sexual) night together in her bed. I was in heaven. To be with someone who loved you was an incredible experience. By the end of the second week, she turned off. Perhaps she knew what I didn't; I never found out. The loss was terrible. We stayed friendly (she was heterosexual, got married, and had lots of children) and never spoke about it.

I kept looking for someone else who might feel as I did, but the lesbians who must have been at Vassar then were very hidden. Sex was not part of my agenda in those days. I had known the facts of sex from an early age, read *Lady Chatterley's Lover* at 12, had a young man court me at 16, but none of this related to me. Sex with men, at that time, just seemed a poor idea, and it didn't occur to me that women could have fun together. I just wanted someone to love and be close to.

In my senior year I somehow got the clue that Djuna Barnes' book *Nightwood* might be of interest. I bought a copy at the Co-op, went down to the small bridge at Sunset Lake and sat riveted through the whole story. What a beautifully written, sad, tormented book. But it said that women did love each other, and I think this was my first step to saying, yes, I am different, I really do love women. It took three more years to come to the final moment of understanding and acceptance.

ANNE MACKAY

The following poem was written for John Malcolm Brinnin's poetry course under the influence of T. S. Eliot. The male sexual imagery was the result of a heavy dose of Joseph Campbell that year, and was not Freudian. I never, ever wanted a you-know-what, but I did have a feminist interest in being a hero.

> *Queen*: To whom do you speak this?
> *Hamlet*:   Do you see nothing there?
> *Queen*: Nothing at all; yet all that is I see.

Involved in careful chairs we smile
At our neurotic friends. I laugh
And rise to claim a cigarette,
Cutting the patterned room in half.

"Well, speak up, woman, what do you know?"
"Oh, nothing from nothing, nothing's new."
Behind the levels of your eyes
The kettle takes its given cue.

While March, disturbing window panes,
(explicit in a snatch of snow)
Slips through the screen, explores the room,
I strain to bend the hero's bow;

Hold hard the solid, ancient wood.
The arrow, notched, convulsed, slants up
Breaks suddenly; a fluid shaft
Curved hissing to the china cup.

The Queen inviolate, the target safe,
We turn to common things, my heart
Scissoring idle sentences
Awaits the signal to depart.

—Vassar, 1947

NAME WITHHELD

*It did show me that perfectly nice
people do such things—not just hairy ogres.*

At Vassar in those days, I didn't know there was such a thing as a lesbian. I'd never heard the word, I don't think, and I'm not even sure I'd ever heard the word homosexual. I was pretty naive. But long before I went to college, as far back as second grade and through my growing up years, I had lots of crushes on girls, and they were intense.

By the time I got to boarding school, my crushes began to have a physical component to them. I had such an urge to touch these young women. There was always lots of hugging, a new and terribly exciting phenomenon for me, and even a stolen and not so innocent kiss or two, but nothing more. I always had the haunting feeling that there was something wrong about all of this—about my desire—and that it was bad.

In my freshman year in Jewett the crushes continued. There was one girl down the corridor that I was crazy about. At night we would all get together in someone's room and hang around and talk—I always tried to sit next to her. She liked me, but didn't get the picture at all. Of course, I didn't get the picture either—I just suffered the guilt of my feelings.

The next year I connected with somebody. We had a lot in common as friends and really enjoyed being together. I don't remember exactly how it started, but I'm sure I was the one who made the first move, and our relationship became physical. It probably started with a back rub. Oh, those back rubs! Anyway, there was some fondling and kissing and once we did what for us would be called "going all the way," still very naive about it all, not acknowledging our feelings to each other, treating it like an adventure or exploration of some kind. We really didn't understand our bodies; we didn't understand what was happening to us physically—what this arousal was all about. I was very emotionally involved, and she was to some extent, too, but I think she was mostly curious. She also had a boyfriend, although I don't think they had had sex at that point.

I had other relationships at Vassar where I would become infatuated and then obsessed with someone. Everything would go along fine until she got the feeling that I was too intense, and then she would back away. I felt rejected and it was very painful.

Of course, I was dating men a lot—we all were. We would visit men's colleges on weekends and have the men come to Vassar. I can't say I enjoyed this at all. The only positive thing about it was the gratification that came from fitting in—and that was important to me. I was also a G-Stringer, and we traveled around singing at different places. I really loved that.

I was very interested in trying to find a guy because this was what was expected. But I knew I was much more susceptible to women than to men. For me, men were to wear on your arm. I picked the good-looking ones. It was strictly for appearances and had nothing to do with their character or personality, which I rarely discovered anyway, due to lack of interest. When they started getting romantically involved with me, I would go along with it for a while. I enjoyed some of their sexual moves, but I was never emotionally involved. The men served a social purpose for me and were very easily replaced, one with another.

It wasn't until my late 20s that somebody brought me out. Although she was quite an attractive person, I had no sexual feelings for her. I think now that may have been because I was hot for yet another straight woman at the time. I *still* didn't know how to use the words straight or gay—I just knew I was intensely preoccupied. Anyway, this gay woman made a pass at me and I was appalled. She was pretty persistent and really forced herself on me. I thought, "Help! What is this? Stop! This is terrible! Get away from me!" She won out, and we had sex, but I was in a daze for days.

SPRING WEEKEND

"This is Mugsy. She comes from California and she's just dying for some real competition."

Drawing by Jean Anderson from *Everything Correlates*, "Some Observations on the Educational Continuum," by Anne Cleveland and Jean Anderson

Our connection didn't work as a lover relationship, but it did show me that perfectly nice people do such things. I mean perfectly *nice* people—not just hairy ogres. It was a real eye-opener for me. It legitimized my feelings. This woman was younger than I, and her college chums slept with each other all the time—a more liberated generation. For her, making a pass at me was no big deal, but it was a very big deal for me.

When I think back on Vassar, I think about it positively. But actually being there, at the LAGA/VC conference, evoked some memories that, strangely enough, surprised me; memories of loneliness and sorrow, a lot of poignant stuff and unhappiness. How different it would have been if I had known more and we were accepted. Only recently I remembered that there was a woman in our dorm who was suspected of being "queer," and how ridiculed she was and cruelly talked and joked about. I hope those days are gone forever at Vassar.

NAME WITHHELD

My friends and I never talked
about our feelings.

When I was at Vassar, I did not identify with being gay or lesbian or homosexual. I had been told that the crushes I had on other girls were a perfectly normal part of growing up. We did talk a lot about queers, but that included teachers and students who were just plain strange. There were lots of those.

Furthermore, when we were involved, my friends and I never talked about our feelings. It remains a mystery how any kind of intimate relationship can occur under these circumstances, but I did have several intimate relationships with special friends while I was in college. Most of these people are now married.

During my four years at school, I dated boys and even got pinned to a nice fellow, but I began worrying because I did not feel anything at all physically for these boys. The obvious reason for the lack of feelings became painfully clear to me when I was in graduate school. There, I had unfortunately gotten obsessed with a nice, straight girl who turned me in to the dean when the affair got too uncomfortable for her. The dean sent me to the school shrink who told me that I was evil—that's how I heard it—and I was asked to leave school. The dean, who was very kind, gave me a medical leave. But the event did nothing for my self-esteem and sent me to the textbooks to read more about inversion. I resolved to be straight and, with the help of a lot of alcohol, lived a very unhappy heterosexual life for two years. I finally gave up and came out in a limited way (because of job security) a few years later. I am still not completely out of the closet because of my job. I did not feel good about being gay until the women's liberation movement came along.

Probably the most painful event in my college life at Vassar occurred when I was a junior. There was a senior in my math class and I really fell hard. Part of it was worship because she was incredibly smart, but there was a great deal of physical appeal. She wore her hair cut very short (like Ingrid Bergman in *For Whom the Bell Tolls*), and like most of us, wore white shirts hanging out over jeans. She let me come over at night when she was working on her thesis and listen to WQXR on the radio. Every other night we'd go for walks on the campus. Sometimes we'd go to the movies. She never made any advances, nor did I. Only once did I get any clue from her that she might be "one of them." When I was in the infirmary, I heard a great stir early one morning. They were bringing in the body of a girl from North that the milkman had discovered. She was not alive; rumor among students was that she had committed suicide because of another woman. The college announced that she had lost her way in the dark and fallen from the window. To my great surprise, my friend was very curious about the whole affair and quizzed me over dinner at Alumnae House.

Our relationship came to an abrupt end one beautiful spring day in the middle of a hike up on the farm. I became overwhelmed with my feelings and blurted out that I loved her. She didn't answer, but gazed off into the distance and asked me what I wanted to do with my life. I was a coward. I could not bring myself to tell her the truth: that I didn't know, that I was terrified, confused by my feelings, and wanted to be like her. Instead, I mumbled the usual bullshit about getting married, etc. She said something about time changing things, and besides, she was graduating shortly anyway. And that was that. We never went on any more hikes and she avoided me. Looking back on it today, I am amazed how little we discussed our feelings in those days. How did we survive? I had alcohol to help me then, but I am so grateful for the openness and freedom of the last 20 years.

NANCY DEAN

I was falling in love with a vision
of what life could be, where
everything was permitted.

I was sitting in a chilly car outside of Avery talking with my former English teacher. It was the spring of 1962, 10 years after my graduation from Vassar. I had been invited back to substitute for Miss Russell, who was very ill, and I'd been asked to teach her Milton seminar. I knew as I listened to this woman of authority, who discussed an "unhealthy clique" that she felt had been running the college, that I was hanging onto the side of a cliff in a high wind, that I was "passing" and that I would hear plenty about the way lesbians were viewed at Vassar, if I didn't faint from anxiety.

I had attended Vassar during the years of the Mellon investigation when "important scientists" stayed at Vassar, subjected the campus to close scrutiny, and discovered to their horror that Vassar was "a matriarchy"—a deplorable state soon to be corrected. My friends grumbled, stating that Yale was a patriarchy and no one thought *that* had to be fixed. But this was before Women's Studies, and some of us still felt apologetic for being women, for writing in a feminine style (a defect for which I was criticized in a writing class at Harvard), for doing things as a woman might do them, instead of correctly, as a man did. Still, one of the great things about Vassar in the palmy days was (and still is, I think) that many of us had the experience of being proud of our gender; we were learning that women could think—within a society that suggested, at least where I had lived, that they couldn't, that being feminine was to be weak-minded, illogical and charming, but defective. Vassar did not teach that doctrine, but here came the Mellon money, supporting scientists who thought that the cure for Vassar's ills (defined by them) was a firmer, more visible male presence.

Vassar, led by remarkable women in crucial positions of power, had presented models of distinguished achievement to its undergraduates. Yet the trustees had called in what the students called "the Melons" to investigate student life at Vassar, and soon the talk about merging with Yale became livelier. I attended Vassar from 1948 to '52, long after the days when first-year women invited seniors to dances where they wore white gloves, long dresses, and filled up their dance cards—as told me by a Vassar alum who taught Art History. Still, in my time, although the outer society was strongly homophobic and one tread very softly in fear of being "reported," the Vassar culture was single-sexed, confident, and proud of the intellectual level at the college. It wasn't until I got into difficulty that I realized that I was to some extent protected by women who were probably my sisters.

As a young woman from a Victorian, patriarchal, and strait-laced family, I found even the privilege of going out to dinner, having a hamburger and martini, without asking permission, heady stuff. In my first few weeks, I met so many women who were brilliant, articulate, and sophisticated that I was "bowled over" as I wrote in letters home. These women seemed so smart; they knew what they thought, what they approved of, what they wanted. I knew what my family said and I believed that was right. One of these women, Anne Reinberg, who had studied Greek and Latin at the Brearley School, went on to major in Classics, do graduate work and then to teach Latin and Greek at Brearley, Yale, and Connecticut College for Women, was dazzling to me. I would come along with one of my father's strongest creeds and she would reduce it to rubble with a few thoughtful questions.

For lesbians, falling in love is often a head trip, I have heard. Perhaps. We talked and talked. I could ask her anything. And she knew all about the ancient Greeks and their views—which meant homosexuality was an approved activity, a loftier love, even. We would start out for the showers in Strong and spend hours sitting on the stairs, still holding our toothbrushes as people passed, saying

"Listen, if *you* want to tell him he stinks in the part,
go ahead — *I'm* taking his seminar next semester."

Drawing by Jean Anderson from *Everything Correlates*, "Some Observations
on the Educational Continuum," by Anne Cleveland and Jean Anderson

"You two still here?" And although "you two" made me nervous,
meaning we were singled out as two together, a warning almost—
still we continued to talk.

Anne was not a college "girl" like me. She was studying, writing
poetry, enjoying dinners with the faculty when her father came up

on weekends—living the life of a displaced adult New Yorker, as it were. Her father would drive up from the city and they would invite one of Anne's teachers out for dinner at one of the more interesting restaurants in the area. The conversation at those dinners—spanning the globe and ranging from McCarthyism, academic freedom, and American activities in South America to Vassar's Mellon Committee—was the most exciting talk I had ever heard. I was falling in love with a vision of what life could be, where everything was permitted, anything was a proper subject for scrutiny, discussion, or art. In my own home at the dinner table, conversation rarely flowed freely and always stopped at some dogmatic position loaded with judgment. "When I speak let no dog bark," I read in Shakespeare and thought it described my father at the dinner table.

So when I fell in love with Anne, I was choosing amazing freedom, iconoclasm even—freedom to question anything. Yet when I realized the erotic element in my feelings for Anne, all those powerful parental rejections surfaced. We had never talked directly about homosexuality, but I remembered:

"You can't be a doctor. Women doctors are all mannish." (Father)

"I don't like smart women." (Father)

"Smart women, like your Aunt Helen, don't know how to make a man happy." (Mother)

"Why do those teachers of yours wear such ugly shoes?" (Mother)

"Degenerates. Unnatural." (Father)

"Those people!" (Mother)

So I promptly became sick, feverish, shaking, weak, and did what my upbringing taught me to do. What I needed was some exercise. I went off to play tennis and ended up in the infirmary with mononucleosis.

Flat on my back, feverish and spacy, I was visited by the Vassar doctor, who strode in looking like a fat Charlton Heston playing Nero. As she walked about my infirmary room, she was part of my nightmare, looking just like those mannish women my father had told me I would become if I went into medicine. Here was the figure out of my future to show me what I would become if I followed my love for Anne. She strode about the room examining the little household objects that Anne had sent up to me: the tiny carpet sweeper, the broom, the little chair and bed that said to me, "I want to live with you." Guiltily, I watched her notice the flowers that Jim, my Merchant Marine friend, had sent me, but she wasn't confused for a minute. "Cute little things." She turned suddenly, "These were sent to you by your roommate?"

"Well, no, she's not my roommate."

"No matter. You know, Nancy, one of the things you have to be very careful of—above all—is intense friendships."

Uh, oh. Where had she gotten that? How did Anne's little toys tell her? I sank deep into the pillows as my fever became a blush of shame. I felt too shaky to cope and just wanted her to leave.

"No one questions us. My friend and I share a house together, but each of us goes her own way and no one questions," she said.

What planet was she on? My friends and I knew nothing about her life, but we all just supposed she was as gay as a hoot owl. She would stride into Avery to give us our freshman hygiene lessons in her white coat, flat thick rubber-soled shoes, husky figure, and clipped hair, and we all figured her knowledge of the female reproductive system was purely theoretical. What did she know about real life: boys or necking in cars? And here she was standing with one hand on her hip, pointing at me with her stubby finger, speaking loud enough for them to hear her in Lathrop telling me—what? You can get away with it if you're careful? I was blocking and couldn't understand. You shouldn't feel intensely! If you do, the relationship is clearly wrong. The sure sign of an unhealthy relationship is intensity.

Now, of course, I shudder at that gruesome lecture: teaching me to numb out and avoid intensity, a code word for passion. But then I was shaking as she left saying she would telephone my father to assure him that I was in good hands. And what did that mean? I was very frightened when I left the infirmary weeks later, and I was determined to stay away from Anne. Fortunately, that resolution went the way of most resolutions, and soon I knew that I couldn't bear *not* to live with her. I felt that if I didn't live with her, we would surely be caught doing something foolish, like my staying in her room at night and having her roommate coming in on us. So after a big discussion, led by Anne's confidence in the reasonableness of Vassar's administrators, we made a formal appeal to the warden to change our living arrangements, which affected two rooming suites, Anne's roommate and mine. We were all interviewed together by the warden in her office and accommodations were made. This was around October of sophomore year, I think.

Anne's evaluation had turned out to be well-founded. Anne had grown to know Vassar's administrators through a terrible event that happened in November of her freshman year, an event that had been spread all over the tabloids with pictures and graphic descriptions. While her father was in Peru on business, her mother, who studied Spanish with a man the Reinberg family had befriended and supported, was strangled by him using her own stockings, as the paper said, before he threw himself in front of a subway train. Pictures, headlines, many crank phone calls—the college protected her from all that. She stayed in her rooms at college and phone calls were diverted and answered by others, until her father could drive up and take her off campus.

Her behavior in all this was amazing to me. She concentrated on her mathematics, did her astronomy, translated Greek. The college locked arms about her and protected her from a crazy world. Perhaps for this reason she felt confident that when she asked for us to live together, she would be treated kindly. She had a reputation as a remarkable student with a 4.0 grade point average and I was a pretty solid citizen as far as anyone knew. Whatever the cause—Anne's reputation, the terrible need anyone would suppose she must have for a close friend, the fact that her father and she often entertained the dean of faculty, a classicist, for dinner and were known as remarkable people—that rooming switch, which could have caused our expulsion if a hostile person had questioned it, went off without a ripple, bureaucratically speaking.

My own roommate, a fine woman whom I hated to hurt, suffered her own disappointment in silence. I never told her that I had fallen in love and couldn't help myself. She never expressed recriminations as she could have. I have always regretted that I could not be open with her and tell her this craziness wasn't "personal."

Anne and I both became tremendously engaged in Vassar life. She was so able as a freshman that she worked as an assistant in the Astronomy lab. She became active in the Curriculum Committee, a group of students and faculty that had lively discussions about college issues and the liberal arts. I became editor of the Vassar literary magazine, active in fencing, hockey, and tennis. Our passionate physical life was mainly expressed on weekends at her apartment in New York, because we were both very afraid of being caught. Yet we were living together. We moved together from

Strong to Main when the seniors had to move as a class, and we were able to share our life in an intimate domestic way, even in a limited physical way, behind a closed door. Since to lock a door would be virtually an admission, we never locked it, but we were greedy for our privacy during those years.

That a person as non-violent as Anne should experience so much violence in her life always seemed—to use one of her favorite words—curious. Although she used to say she was as non-violent as a pillow, she liked to hear about my riding and hunting, which she described as "the pursuit of the uneatable by the unspeakable," in Oscar Wilde's lovely phrase. I have wondered sometimes if the thrill in the dangerous is what drew her. It was about 1967 when a friend called to tell me that Anne had been riding a motorcycle with her second husband in Italy when a large truck roared down a hill and killed them both. She, with all her gifts, and he, a much respected classicist, chair of his department at Yale. I couldn't bear to go to the memorial service at Yale. "Silly," I heard her say. "The memorial won't help me any. It's for you. Teach your class. It's more important." I held my class in Medieval Lit. that evening. I hated to think of a world without her in it.

Pat Wilbert

*Tomorrow I celebrate my 24th year
with my life partner and feel
fortunate indeed.*

I came out as a freshman in the fall of 1948. One of my roommates (there were two) was so concerned that I might be expelled that she suggested I visit the college psychiatrist (a famous shrink who testified at the Alger Hiss trial—Dr. Carl Binger). I convinced her to go in my stead, as she appeared more distraught than I. When she returned from her visit we were both relieved—he had told her not to worry as my expulsion would also require the expulsion of 10% of the student body.

When I was a junior, a senior woman and I got together and later lived in New York City for a while. She is long divorced. She named her daughter after me and we keep in touch. Tomorrow I celebrate my 24th year with my life partner and feel fortunate indeed.

Jewett House (North) *(photo © Anne MacKay)*

PHOEBE SCHOCK

I'm one of the gay grandmothers.

I transferred to Stanford after my sophomore year. Perhaps if I had remained at Vassar, I might have understood my feelings, but I doubt it.

I was in my 40s when I was approached by a younger woman with intimacy in mind. I was overwhelmed. When she and her husband left for England a few months later, she gave me a copy of Kate Millett's *Flying*. That book was quite a contrast to the only information I overheard at Vassar: "Lesbians wear green on Thursdays."

In Drama 105 we read *An Actor Prepares* and were required to do a pantomime on stage. I fought off my stage fright long enough to fill the requirement. When I sat again with the class, Miss Heinlein touched my shoulder. I still remember the current that went through me. That told me that small as my effort seemed, I had accomplished something big for myself.

It wasn't Thursday; however, Miss Heinlein wore a green suit all the time. Maybe she only had one suit? Maybe I was someone who should wear green?

I'm one of the gay grandmothers. I spent most of my life trying to do what was expected of me. After three years in Alcoholics

Anonymous, I realize that though the pressure to do the expected is immense, you do it to avoid responsibility for yourself.

Two, three, more Vassar notes. My godmother, class of 1927, never told me, but reviewing her personal history I would conclude she was a lesbian. The woman I have loved most of my life, who would describe herself as bisexual, is another grandmother, Vassar 1953.

Last spring I visited a member of my class, 1955. One of the first conversations (I was silent) was about poor Smith College—full of deviants. I should have handed her the biography of Elizabeth Bishop I was reading. I didn't as it wouldn't have changed anything.

My ex-husband told our community I left him because I was a lesbian, so I've been out in a sense for 11 years. He also said I had a long-term affair going with our best *man*. Confusion. Fear and confusion.

Jane Rule wrote me once that life is reaching out to other human beings. Thank you for doing that.

P.S. *There is hope in the fear and confusion. A Vassar graduate, another grandmother but not gay, first founded Hospice of Nantucket and now is one of the main workers in our AIDS Network. Reaching out.*

CRISTINA BIAGGI

I felt like a yoyo of ecstasy

and agony.

At Vassar, for the first time in my life, I felt the power and mythic creativity of a community of women. I spent some of the most poignant, glorious, and tearing moments of my life there. Despite all the ups and downs, I always felt the backbone support and the woman-sensitive strength of my friends and classmates. I felt uplifted and inspired by the long tradition of strong sensitive women whose consciousness grew and expanded there and who had the capacity to change the world.

After the initial tremors of being in a new place subsided, my first impression of Vassar was of a physically lush place full of attractive, gifted, and intelligent women—a sort of paradise on earth to a person with my inclinations. As I met more and more interesting women, this feeling of being blissfully "cloistered" in a women's place, constantly stimulated by new and exciting thoughts, became so intense that it was hard for me to concentrate on my studies. I remember bitterly resenting the men from Yale, Amherst *et al*, who invaded the campus on weekends and took some of my cherished women friends away. I found myself longing for Sunday night when we could resume our deep discourses and physical proximity.

At first I too played the "dates" and "weekend" game with men. This proved so meaningless and even harassing in contrast with the wonderful time I had with my friends that I soon gave up any semblance of being sociable with the opposite sex.

The intense feelings of stimulation and excitement at being at Vassar became so acute that I took to acting up. I started hugging and kissing my friends in public and doing other things such as having fencing matches in the hallway of my dorm late at night, wearing a wolfskin and howling like a wolf, flipping peas and other food in the dining room, things that amused my friends but were considered sophomoric by others.

During the middle of my freshman year, one of the senior judges in the student government tried to be helpful. She came to my room and haltingly and in an embarrassed manner told me that if I continued hugging and kissing my friends in public, my actions would be misconstrued. I could be taken for one of those women who (she could hardly get this out) have an unnatural affinity for other women. Since, in my innocence, I didn't fully grasp what she was trying to say, and since I knew about "women who preferred their own sex" (I knew that I did, but I hadn't *categorized* myself as one of those yet), and didn't want to be thought of as sick or unnatural by my peers, I found that I was grateful for her concern. I impulsively reached out and hugged her and said, "Thank you so much for telling me this!" She blushed and quickly backed out of my door muttering, "I just thought I would tell you this."

After this incident, I toned my actions down for a while. The passionate excitement I was feeling had to have an outlet, so I went back to my old ways. I was perpetually in love with this or that woman and my love was always real, deep, and torrid. I never acted upon my desires, however, not because I didn't desperately long to, but because the women I was in love with were ambivalent—they would pull me toward them one moment and push me away the next. I felt like a yoyo of ecstasy and agony.

The culmination of my stay at Vassar took place in the middle of my sophomore year. I had two demerits against me because of lateness and had been grounded on campus, a delightful punishment for me. One of my demerits was acquired when I went to visit one of my inamoratas in her dorm and fell asleep on her couch waiting for her to appear. When she did arrive, it was 1 A.M. After a brief but wonderful interlude with her I tried to sneak back into my dorm. The night watchman, a small, hairy man, intercepted and tackled me, in the process touching me in all the "right" places. I finally yanked myself free, nearly flung him down the stairs, and ran up to my room. The next thing I knew, the white angel (the house supervisor who wore a white uniform) was accusing me of being late and having abused the night watchman.

Then came the straw that broke the camel's back. One Saturday evening my group of friends and I decided to do something out of the ordinary. My sister was visiting me from Mount Holyoke College and I wanted to "show her a good time." We constructed water bombs and dropped them from the third floor windows of Lathrop. One of these bombs (my sister was actually responsible for throwing it) dropped in front of two women, thoroughly splashing them. These women turned out to be President Blanding and a visiting Russian professor who had just given an important good-will talk at the Aula attended by the president and a number of the faculty.

Within minutes, I was apprehended and dragged down to the white angel's office. Of course it was assumed that I was the culprit because of all the other flamboyant things I was constantly doing. Within a short time I was put on trial for my sins and sentenced. It was recommended that I leave Vassar for some time. I was also scheduled to have an interview with the warden and the dean. In all fairness I will add that my grades during my sophomore year left a lot to be desired.

The warden, a no-nonsense, tough-looking woman who talked in a raspy voice and smoked incessantly, leaned menacingly over her desk. She blew a puff of smoke in my face and announced that I had proved myself "unfit for campus life" and that I had to leave Vassar permanently. The dean, who dressed and acted like Jeanette MacDonald, told me the same thing in her patrician manner. These pronouncements affected me as would an expulsion from paradise. I suddenly felt lost and desperate. I felt that I was going to be separated from this sacred enclave of woman power and from my closest passionate friends, my life's blood. On the day of expulsion, my mother came to pick me up and we cried together all the way home.

After this black mark from Vassar, no other college—not even the ones that had wanted me before—would accept me. Finally, the University of Utah (where my mother had connections on the board of trustees) accepted me on the condition that I would behave. I would have to live with my aunt off-campus.

The *coup de grace* from Vassar came the year after my expulsion. I had been attending the University of Utah for nearly a semester. I was doing very well academically and behaving myself socially. My best friend from Vassar, Gail, invited me to come to a Renaissance party she was giving in her room just before Christmas. Everyone would wear costumes and there would be wine—a very dangerous situation.

Unbeknownst to my mother, I left Utah early to go to this party. The party was a wild success! I felt sadder than ever that I was not still at Vassar. Gail had some new, charming, intelligent, beautiful women friends who attended the party. We danced with elan, we flirted wildly, we drank copiously, we talked passionately about lofty subjects—everything that one does at the best of parties. I felt enamored of most of the women there and I felt that my feelings were reciprocated.

Finally it came time to break up. I decided to walk one of my new inamoratas home to her dorm. In her room we started kissing when I suddenly realized, like Cinderella, that I should get back to Gail's dorm. I dashed back but found that I had been locked out. I tried to sneak into Main but was apprehended. Gail came downstairs to explain that I was staying with her, but, because of my unfit-for-campus-life status (which seemed still to be very fresh in the administration's eyes), I was told I could not stay on campus but had to go to Alumnae House at once. I did not accept that, and in a dramatic scene where I had to forcibly yank myself away from the campus guard who was holding me, I escaped and ran out of Main. I hid under Gail's window and howled like a wolf. I knew that she or her friends would know who it was and would let me in. Soon someone came and I spent the night in Gail's room as planned.

The next morning the dean strongly reprimanded Gail, telling her that if she ever harbored me again she would be expelled. She was campused for a time. As for me, the dean said she would write to my mother to tell her of the incident. I was henceforth considered *persona non grata*, and if I ever set foot on Vassar soil again, I would be legally prosecuted.

This was the final blow, and I did not go to Vassar again until I visited briefly 10 years later when the men had just colonized the campus. By then I had married, had had two children, gotten divorced, and was involved in a long-term relationship with a woman.

Twenty-five years later, some of my classmates sent me an invitation to our 25th reunion. It was with extreme bitter-sweet pleasure that I attended that fabulous weekend. It was cathartic to be completely out and totally honest, at long last, about everything in my life without being judged or indicted.

GAIL ELLEN DUNLAP

We were delirious with the

atmosphere at Vassar; the great trees

and the beauty.

From a tape made on May 26, 1991.

I came to Vassar in the fall of 1955 knowing I was a lesbian. Although I was inexperienced in sexual matters, I knew I preferred the company of women to all else, except maybe animals. I had found among my great aunt's books a copy of Sappho's poetry, so I knew I wasn't alone, although it seemed that 2,000 years was a long stretch for sisterhood.

I came from a farm in the Midwest where my social life was bland. I had spent a lot of time reading poetry and I was very romantic. I was also shy and extremely modest and thought I'd probably live a very reclusive life. I was totally unprepared for what was to happen to me at Vassar.

As a freshman I lived in Lathrop. I felt like an outsider, but I was wide-eyed. I'd chosen Vassar after all because it was a women's college, and the campus and the curriculum were enchanting to me. Almost immediately I met Cristina, who lived across the hall and was one of the lucky ones who had a room of her own. Since I stayed up late at night and she stayed up late at night, we found ourselves talking, talking, and talking. We were delirious with the atmosphere at Vassar; the great trees and the beauty. We were 17. We soon discovered a Sapphic affinity and because we were both so athletic and healthy we were soon engaged in many exploits: we'd swim in the lake or sneak into the Chapel basement which was filled with classical statues. In the moonlight Cristina seemed to me a veritable goddess, Artemis or Athena. We were both in love with all things Greek, and she was so much more than I, it seemed—she was so exuberant and outgoing and fearless. Sometimes I don't know how I lived through that first year because I didn't sleep very much. Looking back, I think I learned everything about my heart then and about passion and about betrayal. Certainly it was growing up in a kind of paradise with all the other girls around and those wonderful teachers. Except for those restrictions and the late-night curfews, we were absolutely free and my heart bloomed.

The Christmas of my first year when I went home, my father received two arctic wolf skins from a crony of his. I took them back with great excitement to Vassar. When Cristina saw them she was very excited too and we put them on and wore them. Sometimes at night we would go outside and howl at the moon. We did these things in all innocence, but it wasn't to last.

Early in our sophomore year, Cristina was expelled without much explanation. It was so sudden and so violent, I was grief-stricken. I remember for weeks not being able to see very well because of the tears in my eyes. Our other friends were dismayed and we did have interviews with the president and the head of her department to find out why, but it was to no avail. She came back furtively on weekends to see all of us, but of course it wasn't the same.

At that time I had a lead part in Soph Party. The drama was about Olympian gods who came to earth, and the character I played fell in love with a mortal girl. I was so convincing in the part that suddenly there were other girls interested in me in ways that went beyond normal friendships. When I say normal friendship, I don't really know what I mean, except that in the 1950s, homosexuality was considered unnatural, a mental disease, and punishable by law. This, after all, was the era of McCarthyism and compulsive heterosexuality, so I was wary.

Now I was on my own and I had some reputation from the play. I was often an extra in the Drama Department productions and had great fun choosing costumes from the costume room. My girlfriends were all artistically inclined and there were quite a few of us, although the word "lesbian" was never, or very rarely, mentioned.

I remember one incident with a lover who was very self-confident.

We had gone to the movies at the Juliet theater and held hands a lot. I wore a cape in those days which concealed our hands. As we walked back to the campus, a group of boys from the town stopped and tried to pick us up. She turned and yelled at them, "Go away! Leave us alone, we're lesbians!" I myself was shocked, but very, very happy.

I was part of many groups, and I had older friends who helped me choose classes and educated me about music and books. Oh, the books I found! There was Djuna Barnes, Virginia Woolf, Jeanette Foster, Radclyffe Hall, Simone de Beauvoir, and Gertrude Stein. I didn't like *The Well of Loneliness*, and I certainly didn't like the popular dyke literature. My trips to the gay bars in New York rather frightened me. I couldn't identify with those brave souls who were out at that time. I suppose I had too much middle-class background and shied away from the heavy butch/femme role-playing.

However, at Vassar, my lesbian life was quite full. There were times when I realized that I was the center of jealousies and rivalries and that I was quite popular. But as I said, there was no lesbian community as such, though there were some of us who seemed to be threads connecting separate groups of women. I would hear of lesbian activity and narrow escapes and so forth, but I never witnessed anything overt (except myself).

By the beginning of my junior year I had been to Europe and had the Grand Tour and I seemed to be a woman of the world. My studies were good and I was ready to have a love affair, an obsessive, clandestine, all-consuming love affair. Which I did. It was difficult really. There were no locks on the doors and we could have been caught at any time—and almost were. There was also a lot of drinking and craziness and my emotions were uncontrollable. I'd lost my distance.

The summer after my junior year I went to Greece with Cristina. This was a culmination of many dreams that we'd had and was absolutely life-changing. When I returned to Vassar in the fall with my thesis looming over my head, I was in a different frame of mind and quite unsettled. My love affair was over, having ended in a great deal of pain on both sides. I felt I had to get down to serious academic work. But I was totally unfocused and also drinking too much, and I began to get in trouble with the authorities. I had planned a great fete, we called it the Renaissance Party, and all my friends from the different groups were invited. Cristina was coming from Utah. We had wine, we had delicacies, and everyone got very drunk. Cristina was apprehended by a night watchman and there was damage to property. The next morning, the warden's secretary knocked on my door and told me I was expected in her office immediately. The warden told me there was really not much reason to return after Christmas vacation. Later, the warden, Sarah Gibson Blanding, and I sat in a darkening office on a cold evening while the warden blew cigarette smoke my way and Miss Blanding said that if I didn't relate the names of my friends to her (she had a legal pad handy), they would fix it so that I could not be accepted in any college or university in the U.S. *ever.* I left without saying their names.

All vacation I waited for the telegram to my parents, whom I had told about the party. They were supportive and I think puzzled (they didn't really know what had happened to me since I'd gone to Vassar), and allowed me to go back to Vassar and face the music. As a result of the ensuing student government "trial," I was suspended for two weeks and spent the time with a Vassar graduate in New York City.

It was deep winter when I went back. I was way behind in my classes and I had my thesis to do. I was really at loose ends and the next thing I knew I was involved in a traffic accident with two other Vassar girls in a car that was illegal (the college did not allow students to have cars). With that, the curtain really fell. One of us was hurt and we spent that night in a motel. The next morning the local press had been alerted and we were chauffeured back to the campus and more or less hidden in the infirmary until the student government trial took place. We were all three expelled, which seemed unfair, since we were hardly able to defend ourselves. I want it to be clear that, although I was charged with breaking the rules concerning alcohol and automobiles, those rules were changed the year I left. I think the trouble was caused by having to live a secret life (although that had its mysterious appeal at times) and feeling guilty, degenerate, and unnatural.

During both trials there was great pressure put on me to divulge the names of my friends. I didn't have to do that because my friends volunteered to meet with the president and the warden at tea, and every one of them came to the second trial. I was expelled for a year, but was given the opportunity to return if I visited a psychiatrist regularly for a year. I did that and also went to Harvard summer school and got A's. I was readmitted in the spring of 1960, but there

Wolf Girls. Gail Ellen Dunlap *(right)* and Cristina Biaggi, Halloween, 1956. *(photo © Marianne Buchenhorner)*

were lots of changes by then. On the day I got back I had an appointment with Dr. Nixon, the school psychiatrist, who told me in no uncertain terms that there was a circle of women who were prepared to sit at my feet, and I think he said "worship me." I didn't know how to take this and supposed it was a warning so I was on my best behavior, but I missed my friends. There had been a clearing out of everyone who was suspected of being lesbian. It was also then that President Blanding said to me that, "Cristina has been expelled because she was unfit to live in a social community."

I tried to be discreet, but it was difficult. I got love letters, I got congratulatory notes through the unstamped mail, I got flowers in my room, little gifts outside my door, whispered messages in the dark, and young women in various states of inebriation would surprise me when I'd come back from the library. I was walking a tightrope, under surveillance at all times. I made new friends and there was much support from students, and my teachers were extremely kind. I graduated in 1960, but after that I was really quite numb and bereft, because I didn't understand what had been done to us all, and there was so much tragedy and separation. Most of my friends married. Cristina had married and everyone was scattered. For many years, in fact until recounting this and remembering, I have been very bitter and hurt, and unable not to cast blame. But with remembering I feel healed.

Also, I have had a good life. I stopped drinking and I met many women in the women's movement. I've had the companionship and devotion of another Vassar woman, Charoula, for 29 years. The farm that we are regenerating organically is lesbian land and a wildlife sanctuary. My reunions have been wonderful since I've come out. Everything for me is working out splendidly now!

There wasn't much to help us as lesbians at Vassar in the 1950s, and we were ashamed and afraid of the truth about ourselves. Some of us are dead now, but I would like to extend my support and my affection to all the young lesbians at Vassar today.

BETSY CROWELL

Rumor had it that they danced nude

under the moon . . . and that they

were lesbians.

I deliberately chose a women's college. At 12 I said it was because of the article I read in *Holiday* magazine about Smith. They had horseback riding there. Later on, when I chose Vassar sight unseen over Smith, I said it was because of Vassar's superb Philosophy Department. By then I knew that I wanted to be with women, only women, where all my best times had always been. I knew then that my friendships with women were completely satisfactory. The sexy buzz was an extra. My high school sweetheart was also going to Vassar. We came East to Vassar with each other and our mothers and ended up in dorms across the quad from each other.

When I think back on that first year at Vassar, what I recall most was the richness and the vibrancy of the place. Somehow we had escaped from the ghastly 1950s out there and discovered another world of incomparable sharing and support. The college was governed by an all-woman team, with Sarah Gibson Blanding and Florence Wislocki foremost in the hierarchy. All around us were impressive, strong, feisty, smart, and very respectable women who had made it on their own and, some of us suspected, with each other. Incredibly, I cannot recall ever discussing this flat-footed observation with anyone. The fact was that most of us had passionate friendships at Vassar and few of us ever dared to acknowledge their importance to each other. The "L" word was rarely uttered. My roommate did tell me that if I were a man she would marry me. That's about as close as we ever came to wrapping words around our love for each other.

There was one period of time, though, when I recall the utter terror of being labeled a lesbian. As a house officer I could not fail to notice who came and went and with whom at what time of day. And what I noticed most that year was a certain group of women from different classes and dorms, who came and went together. Rumor had it that they danced nude under the moon in bedsheets and that they were lesbians. They were some of the smartest and surely the most interesting women in my class. I liked their nerve: they stayed out after hours, signed in for each other, and thumbed their noses at the administration and the rest of us. Not one of them wore a pageboy haircut and several were knockouts.

Then, quite without warning, several of them mysteriously left the college mid-year. A witch-hunt, albeit a quiet one, was whipping through the place. We heard that the trustees had been told that Vassar was a hotbed of lesbianism and that the papers were about to go public with the news. A good friend of mine suddenly left. Mononucleosis, they said. Years later she told me she fled after she had been hauled before the administration and accused of kissing someone good night in front of her door. As she described it, this was a strictly social kiss. One wonders how many women simply left for fear of the sort of scrutiny that must have been undertaken by the administration. There were rumors of spies among us and friends accusing friends. It was during this purge that we did discuss our own fears about our feelings with women. My recollection of those conversations is of the unspeakable self-hate we felt. I was engaged to be married at the time and held onto that respectable straw of normality for dear life. My roommate and my high school friend both became engaged several months later. We did marry and between the three of us we have nine children, four husbands, and to my knowledge, two female lovers, both mine.

I know little of what became of the women who danced by the light of the Vassar moon. During the past 20 years, as I have lived with another woman and raised my children, I've thought many times about Vassar and all those Vassar women. I'm sure that the Seven Sisters colleges with women who loved women at the helm were the first to undertake such vile purges, springing as they usually do from a position of hidden self-loathing. There was too much to lose. Can any of us imagine a lesbian witch-hunt at a coeducational Vassar? And will I ever find out what really became of my closest friends? It is sad for me to realize that I was one of the lucky survivors and that so many of the women I knew at Vassar who had deeply loving and passionate attachments with other women probably never allowed themselves that wild freedom of self-discovery and affirmation. It has been very difficult for my two closest friends at Vassar to know that I live with a woman in such gladness. They've been angry and confused and don't want to talk about it. I think I understand why, but it doesn't make me feel any better. Maybe they'll be late bloomers, like the woman I met the other day who has been loving another woman for 10 years and who had never met a lesbian couple, as far as she knew. A mutual friend suggested that she sit down and talk with me. We met for a quiet lunch at the Museum of Modern Art. As we talked about our lives, children, and work, and discovered that we were both Vassar alumnae, it was plain to see that for her this meeting was going to be pretty close to an epiphany. As we parted, she asked for my reassurance that I would say nothing to reveal her identity and that I introduce her and her lover to other women. I'll do that and hope for the best.

NAME WITHHELD

My hunger to know starved.

My paranoia flourished.

Shit! I lived on the corner of the first floor in Cushing. I had selected Cushing because I thought being separate from Joss (party) and the quad (safe) would attract less conforming, more individualistic people.

Down the hall lived some women who intensely interested me. I was terribly afraid to find out about them by directly asking anyone. That would arouse suspicions about me. I'd be branded and thought of as queer by everybody. I'd never recover from the shame. Somebody said they cooked stuff in their room and had long hair. Were they ancient language majors? That's all I ever knew. These two women down the hall—what were they like, what did they do, talk about, wear, look like? My hunger to know starved. My paranoia flourished.

I was developing a friendship with a music major. After a year and a half, I touched her foot and she gave me a knowing look that said, "I don't go for *that* or you in *that* way." We were going to live on the same wing at Cushing our junior year but we both left. I flunked out and she transferred to a Midwestern university.

I learned nothing about gay life at Vassar. I was too afraid to accept myself and blocked my own way for a long time. It wasn't until I'd graduated from art school, five years later, that *it* happened.

Vassar College Library *(photo © Anne MacKay)*

LUCY CROSS

*Nothing has gone wrong with me. I
know that. This is what's really the
difference between now and when I
was in college.*

Excerpts from a speech at the LAGA/VC Conference, April 13, 1991.

I wanted to go to Vassar because of the good choir and the good
Drama Department, but what really clinched it was when I went
for my interview and some friends told me about the Wolf Girl—
somebody who put on a wolf skin and went howling around the
Circle in the full moon. That's me, I thought. There's room for me!

My mother went to Vassar. She was very concerned that all
her children should function vigorously toward the betterment of
society. Of course we know there were lesbians here in the 1930s.
Mary McCarthy wrote *The Group*, so we should know that.

Homosexuality is nothing you can choose. I don't think any
adolescent would ever choose it. I wanted desperately *not* to be. Are
things different now?

Of course, I know now that something is very right for me about
being gay. Not having that choice has given me some other choices;
it's given me resilience, even intelligence, because I'm forced to deal
with truths that others choose to deny. Nothing has gone wrong
with me. I know that. This is what's really the difference between
now and when I was in college. I spent six years going to a psychiatrist trying to learn not to be gay. You know what one said? "It's
attributable to some aberration in your psychosexual development."

Tripe! But that's what we knew about it, it was arrested development.

Everybody knew I was gay before I did. I found out what people were saying when a boy I was flirting with at a prom told me that someone had pointed me out to him as a "switch-hitter." It was rumored that there was a lesbian ring centered in Cushing mostly, which was where I lived. They called it the Zoo—did you, too? So my friends asked me about it, assuming I would know. In fact, there were some girls who got called to the president's office for disciplinary action, but my personal perception was that these were the same girls who were experimenting with mind-altering substances, and that the discipline had as much to do with that as anything else. The only thing I can tell you for sure about that lesbian ring is that I was never invited. I wonder if the Wolf Girl knows? It didn't occur to me to try to make contact with other girls who loved girls. In fact, we rather tried to avoid each other. Who knows, if you made friends with one, it might mean that you accepted that you were one. I had one friend, she really was and still is a friend, but we never talked about anything in college. I guess she tried, once or twice, but I couldn't imagine identifying with her. She was butch and I was going to grow up. About three days before graduation we went out together for some steamed clams, and we did finally have a real exchange at that late date, and I realized to my great sorrow what I'd missed.

Is Vassar still a place you go if you want to be a Wolf Girl? My niece is at Smith and she said to my shock, "I wouldn't have considered Vassar." "Why not?" "It went coed. It's so difficult to relate well to other women when there are men around."

Please tell me it's not so!

A note added by Lucy Cross:

> *The best part of this presentation, for me, was the appearance afterward of three young women with hands extended, one of whom announced enthusiastically, "Hi! We're Wolf Girls!"*

CHAROULA (JOY) DONTOPOULOS

. . . a paradisial time of swims in
cool creeks, garlanded feasts in the
Vassar woods, moonlit nights
listening to her playing the
guitar . . .

Five years ago, at our 25th reunion, I wrote a statement in which I thanked Vassar for making me a lesbian! Though that sounded somewhat ironic, it was nevertheless absolutely true—my gratitude was sincere, in other words. The irony lay in the fact that Vassar—that is, the college with its hierarchy, its unfair laws, and absurd moral strictures—would have me, and others like me, singled out and punished for loving women. But Vassar—the then unique all-women's community, the romantic setting, the wonderful women teachers, the amazing new knowledge contained in the myriad of books at the library—all that gave me the freedom and inspiration to find out who I truly was.

I arrived at Vassar in the late '50s in what I later realized was the suffocating aftermath of the McCarthy years. I was a foreign student from Greece, the land of Sappho, but with very little actual knowledge of Sapphic love, though plenty of unexplained feelings for women. (Note: I came in as a sophomore, because the extensive curriculum of Greek schooling allowed me to skip a year.)

During my first semester, reports of two girls caught by the white angel in the act of making love with each other inflamed my imagination. The friend who reported this to me said that women like that were called lesbians.

The word sent shivers through my entire being. It illuminated the darkest corners of my soul and clarified certain salient facts about my personality which had perplexed me all along, such as my distinct desire to be with my girlfriends, when they instead wanted to be with their boyfriends.

So I was a lesbian! This new knowledge filled me with immense excitement, as well as dread and anxiety. What next? The two girls were immediately expelled, and this was what would happen to me, too, if I put my sexual preferences to practice. Besides, how on earth did anyone find other lesbians at Vassar? Considering the harsh punitive consequences, who in their right mind would openly admit they were lesbians and open to contact?

Well, it wasn't easy. I was to find out that the lifestyle I had discovered to be mine could only exist illicitly. No one much trusted anyone else, especially a freshly arrived and possibly naive foreign student on scholarship who spoke English with difficulty and understood others with even greater difficulty! Those with lesbian tendencies mostly lived in isolation from each other, or came together in unspoken, implied ways. This could be very exciting and intoxicating in one respect. In another, it led to incredible frustration and a feeling of near schizophrenia. I suspect that this was the reason those of us so inclined drank a lot and acted pretty wild a lot of the time. Under the influence of alcohol, at night, we felt free to exalt in one another's company, to dance with each other, laugh, recite poetry, listen to music, and—the bravest of us—make love with each other. Sober, in the daytime, we tried to be the good girls training to be the good wives the administration wanted us to become.

Soon after the incident of the double expulsion, I met a girl who seemed to me to be at the center of a hub of romantic intrigue and clandestine activity. I was highly fascinated by her and sought her out wherever she went, in and out of campus, which was mostly Card's, a very disreputable bar in those days. However madly I sought her out, though, she remained remote and mysterious. I met and made friends with most of her friends and entourage, but never with the queen herself—not until my senior year.

Once, toward the end of my sophomore year, after pursuing her to Card's and finding her as aloof as ever, I drank too much and did some crazy exhibitionist dancing, which the next day left me with a strong hangover and a sense of deep mortification. I felt I had behaved badly because I was so confused about my feelings toward this girl. I decided I needed professional assistance. I stupidly called and made an appointment with the school psychiatrist. After I told him my confusion around being a lesbian, he proceeded to ask me whether my feelings had to do with anyone specific. To my amazement, he mentioned the name of this girl and told me to watch out, that she was the center of a dangerous circle, and that I should stay away from her. It sounded like a threat, and the thought occurred to me that I had better behave or else my scholarship might be endangered.

For the next year or so, I tried hard to suppress all my lesbian feelings. This effort was punctuated by a series of incidents involving girls who I knew had lesbian tendencies. These incidents usually ended in expulsion. The reasons given were drunkenness, suicide attempts, etc., but I knew deep down that the bottom line was that these girls were lesbians. To be a lesbian was sick, unnatural. The message was: shape up or ship out. So I tried to shape up.

This wasn't easy either. It became clearer and clearer who was sleeping with whom. I went to parties where lesbian activity was obvious. One of my closest friends had an affair with the so-called "center of the dangerous circle," and I myself fell madly in love with another close and unsuspecting friend whom I couldn't bear to burden with my illicit feelings.

By the beginning of my senior year, it was impossible to pretend to myself anymore, and to go through the charades of dates with boys and other such nonsense. The happiest times I had at Vassar were weekdays, when the campus was full of women, and nothing but women. My unhappiest moments were the weekends when most girls would go off on dates or men would invade our community. I hated them.

Exhausted by my unrequited love, I turned toward more tangible areas, namely, my first fascination, whom at least I knew to be a lesbian. Though she and I never made love while at Vassar, we became extremely close. My happiest memories are of gallivanting around Vassar either alone with her or with other friends who were like us. Spring of my senior year—all the way up to graduation— was a paradisial time of swims in cool creeks, garlanded feasts in the Vassar woods, moonlit nights listening to her playing the guitar and crooning in her sweet melancholy voice.

Oh, the ecstasy and pain of love!

Though she and I ended up making love a couple of times after

Maria Mitchell Observatory *(photo © Anne MacKay)*

graduation, this relationship was to remain most romantic, highly intense but platonic. She, however, introduced me a year later to Gail Ellen Dunlap '59, one of the "Wolf Girls," who became and has remained my partner for the past 29 years. Gail, this other girl, and friends of Gail's such as Christina Biaggi '59, have been at the very center of my life throughout the years.

So again, I thank Vassar for facilitating my meeting these wonderful women, as well as all my beloved roommates, whose lifestyles led them away from me, but who have remained beloved nevertheless. Without them, my life simply wouldn't have been the same.

BEVA EASTMAN

The college atmosphere was
extremely judgmental and punitive.

Recently, I attended a presentation at the college where I am an associate professor. The presenter, a woman of color, talked about the large alumnae recruitment networks that exist at her college (Smith). However, the one group that does not participate in these alumnae recruiting efforts are the women of color, who attend Smith, graduate, use that diploma as a method of entrance into their careers, but do not "bond" to the college as they pass through. The reason for the lack of bonding is the "stuff" that happens to them during their four years, better known as the campus climate or culture.

In many ways, Smith is now addressing the "stuff" that makes up the daily life on a college campus in order to create a supportive environment for all of its students. As I listened to the Smith representative, I responded inwardly, understanding why I, although a white woman, had not bonded to Vassar.

I arrived at Vassar and immediately experienced the feeling of "being other." Practically the first question my assigned roommate asked me was about my debutante party. I maintained some sense of credibility with her only by explaining that women made their debuts the last year of college in the society culture of my state, never admitting to her that for two reasons I would not be making my debut: I was a lesbian and I came from a tradition of social change that looked upon debutantes as a cultural anachronism.

I also grew up with an alcoholic mother and a father enmeshed in her drinking. The summer before I entered Vassar, my mother and I returned early from the summer vacation. She was to help me gather the clothes and necessary items to move 2,000 miles to Vassar. However, my mother started drinking so heavily that she thought she was dying. She became so frightened that I spent the time taking care of her and arrived at Vassar very scattered.

The first semester of my freshman year I was asked in my English class to write a paper on families. We were to compare and contrast the family in the novel we were reading with our own. So, I presented the situation of an alcoholic family system. However, when I met with the instructor in one of those required individual sessions, the paper was dismissed completely with the statement, "Well, this assignment did not work for everyone," and the professor and I continued our session by "discussing" the novel.

Since I advise and work with college students continually, I recognize now that the professor was not able to handle the issues that I had raised. But at the time, his treatment only added to my sense of self as different. College as a place to grow both intellectually and emotionally and develop into a whole person instead of splintered facades was not my experience. Survival at Vassar became for me a disassociated, intellectual mind set in which college life and classes were in one box, my family life was in another, and any private living ran underground somewhere.

I spent my junior year abroad, because by my sophomore year I was close to a nervous breakdown due to the campus culture. I had tried different methods to become comfortable there—leadership roles, community service, and different subgroups. True, there was a lesbian subculture on the campus, both with the students and with the faculty, but I was too fearful to seek it out.

The college atmosphere was extremely judgmental and punitive. During my sophomore year, one of my roommates was asked to leave because she had married. Also, the senior class president, three months before she was to graduate, was expelled since she had married. I knew my family was not going to support me after graduation and I needed the diploma in order to find a job. Therefore, I ran from any possible friendship or situation that could lead to intimacy. If straight class presidents could be expelled, what might happen to me? Suppose I was expelled or someone wrote a letter that prevented me from being employed?

I was not able to make contact with the faculty subculture. I went to dinner at a faculty home my sophomore year with the eager expectation of hearing about the lives of two women faculty I admired. When the evening opened with a discussion of Milton's shell imagery, I knew that we were going into academic hiding and would not be open with each other. However, I was and am still most grateful for the women faculty who helped me through some bureaucratic messes and in particular to one woman who suggested that I join the Junior Year Abroad program.

The predominant student culture at that time expressed the Vassar cultural values that a woman was to be educated to be a wife and community volunteer. Although there were plenty of single women faculty and administrators on campus, they were dismissed by students as possible role models—"that is not the *real* life." I did not experience faculty as interested and available for students, and my friends thought that you were odd if you wanted to become friends with a faculty member.

My senior year at Vassar was most strange, for I spent the fall deliberately breaking many regulations and acting out. After a year of living abroad in Munich, Germany, most of the restrictions on life at Vassar seemed archaic (by now, all those regulations have been abolished). I know now that my acting out was the way I relieved my anger. One day, a friend came in to report that two women down the hall had been found in bed together. We discussed the implications calmly (would they be expelled?), while inwardly I churned with envy for their freedom and anger at the possible expulsion.

My last semester was spent working on my thesis and hiding even more. I had met two Vassar graduates who were lesbians and living in New York. They "adopted" me, arranged for my first job, helped me find a place to live, and even lent me a sailboat that summer. However, my eagerness to be with them had to be hidden from my roommates. I remember to this day denying to a roommate my interest in these women, and it became the final split between me and Vassar. My life as a lesbian and my life at Vassar could not coexist. After graduation I drove down the road from Main to the

Main Building *(photo by Dixie Sheridan/Courtesy of Vassar College)*

campus entrance yelling with joy for "getting out and away." I felt that I finally could start my life as I wanted and could shed the emotional isolation of those four years.

Recently, at my state college with over 9,000 students and about 300 faculty, we reinstated a Freshman Seminar to help students explore and acknowledge the transition from high school to college. My years at Vassar serve me well as a negative role model, one that I do not want my students to experience. College does not have to be a place where students are "molded" for a particular life or where one voice, instead of many voices, is heard.

However, the heterosexism on my campus is fierce. I know that I would like to lead less of a "split" life, so I push at the edges every now and then. A joyful vision would be that all of us—students, faculty, administrators, and staff—could continue our personal development along with our intellectual growth and that the entire academic community might feel enriched by listening to the many different voices and delight in that diversity.

ELLEN SHER-BIERHORST

My Vassar years were terribly dark,
cold, and lonely.

Mother of three and bloodied veteran of a 20-year marriage, I have spent the last three years in life partnership with a woman.

When I was at Vassar, from 1958 to 1962, during the presidency of Sarah Gibson Blanding, lesbianism was so scary that in all our endless, courageous, and iconoclastic talk sessions, the subject never even came up! Looking back, I see invisible rivers of sexual attraction pouring down the corridors and sloshing through the rooms. I certainly see my own clear attraction for the dark corridor mate freshman year, my hot crush on the sophisticated New Englander sophomore year, my wild feelings for my philosophy professor, and on and on.

My Vassar years were terribly dark, cold, and lonely. Looking back now, I am appalled and angry at the prohibition against friendliness, against warmth, let alone love. I had picked Vassar because of an alumna's testimonial of a warm, vibrant, and "real" experience in the "Prexy" years [Henry Noble McCracken—retired 1946]. But I found myself bewildered and depressed in a community where anything less than complete detachment was considered unthinkably gauche.

Could it be that it was homophobia that had clamped off the warmth of the whole campus? Could it be that the assemblage of all that female power and beauty was just too stimulating, too terrifying for everyone, and so we all shied away lest our convent-like isolation and our pounding hormones lead to *feelings*—or, heaven help us, *acts*? One hypothesis is that constriction of spirit during this era at Vassar was precisely because there was an unmarried woman in the presidency. Certainly "Prexy" seemed to be everybody's beau during his golden era, providing a kind of bridegroom to legitimize the heterosexuality of the college as a whole. Perhaps during the Blanding years Vassar felt herself, unconsciously, to be a single woman, embarrassed by the faint shadow of suspicion on her sexual normalcy and so, inhibiting the free flow of a naturally more robust, frolicking, and warm nature.

Today, my daughter is a senior at tiny, Quaker, Earlham College in Indiana. I can't help but envy the freedom of the students to be warm! They are affectionate with each other, passionate about studies, and social issues. And the liveliest club on campus is the LBGPU (Lesbian, Bisexual, and Gay People's Union).

NAME WITHHELD

*I felt alienated from the rest of my
class and have been back to reunion
only once. . . .*

I had always thought of myself as heterosexual, but often said that I wanted to experience a lot of different things. At the time, I hadn't experienced much of anything.

Toward the end of my junior year, a friend from one of my classes was studying with me in my room. She purposely stayed beyond curfew, so that we slept together. She told me later that she thought I was gay. In fact, this was my first experience making love. I knew that I was gay that night. However, I couldn't accept what this meant for my life. The next morning I was distraught and went to see Dr. Nixon, the school psychiatrist. I had cut myself and knew that the situation would be repeated if I saw this woman again. The solution was that I was admitted to the infirmary and my mother was called to take me home. I had asked Dr. Nixon not to tell my mother why I had to leave. Many years later, I learned he had told her. She never has discussed my homosexuality with me, nor I with her.

The following September, I returned to Vassar, after a summer of seeing a psychiatrist, with the proviso that I continue psychotherapy while completing my senior year.

Senior year I had lovers, saw the psychiatrist, and graduated. One lover was a sophomore who had never been involved with a

Main Building hung with a banner for the LAGA/VC Conference, April 1991 *(photo © Anne MacKay)*

woman before our relationship. Emotionally, she was falling apart. When I told her that our relationship was over because I couldn't handle her problems as well as mine, she decided to drop out of school. In the morning, I woke up and she had cut her arms with a razor about 10 times and the bed was covered in blood. I drove her home to her parents and never saw her again.

My next lover was also basically straight. We lived most of the time in her room. Her roommate was my first lover and she had a non-student woman lover living with her for most of the year. This relationship ended when I refused to drive the three of them to Florida for spring vacation. My lover went back to her boyfriend.

My friends knew I was gay and accepted it, but I knew that these friendships would not be long-lasting once college was over. In fact, I only communicate with one person from college on an ongoing basis. I felt alienated from the rest of my class and have been back to a reunion only once (the 25th) for part of one day.

Had there been a gay/lesbian organization at Vassar when all this was happening, I think I might have been better able to handle my own coming out and found friendship and companionship. The feeling of being alone, certain that rejection would be the response of my friends, and not knowing where to find another gay person to be a friend or lover, made accepting myself a lot harder. After college, I tried being straight with 15 years of therapy while living in gay relationships.

I still look for the names of my ex-lovers in the *Quarterly* class notes. My first lover writes about her husband, children, and career. I wrote once about my job, education, and pastimes. So I'm still in the closet to some extent, although my family, my employer, and fellow employees know I live with a woman.

NANCY S. ERICKSON

I thought that, by and large,

women were nicer to be with than

men, so I could understand why

some women would want to be

lesbians.

I want to let you know what it was like for me to be a *heterosexual* student at Vassar in the late '60s, when no one was talking about lesbianism, but everyone was whispering about it.

I was a transfer student in the fall of 1965, in my junior year. At the end of that year I heard that Cushing had single rooms available, so I applied and got in. When I arrived in the fall and told a few of my friends where I was living, one person said with surprise, "That's where they put all the lesbians." It didn't matter to me, particularly because I had little respect for many of my heterosexual fellow students, who seemed to spend all their time and money trying to impress men who didn't seem worth impressing. I thought that, by and large, women were nicer to be with than men, so I could understand why some women would want to be lesbians. (That did not explain why men would want to be homosexual, of course.)

I sincerely hope that things are better for homosexual students at Vassar now than they were when I was a student there. I had feared that things might actually get worse after Vassar went coed. There were rumors that a large percentage of the male students who went to Vassar in those early years were homosexual, and I was afraid that some people at Vassar would want to push them back into the

Chapel *(photo by Dixie Sheridan/Courtesy of Vassar College)*

closet in order to protect the reputation of the college. Apparently, this repression did not occur, or if it did, the repression itself was kept hidden.

Anti-gay and anti-lesbian acts of discrimination harm not only the intended victims, but all of us.

Karin L. Abbey

These women simply knew that they
loved me and that I needed them.

At the end of the summer before my sophomore year at Vassar,
I fell in love. Not that I recognized it as such—the idea that I could
fall in love with a woman had not occurred to me. My best friend
from high school introduced me to her new friend from summer
camp and I was entranced. We saw each other (the three of us) twice
more before I went back to school. Then this new friend and I wrote
to each other. Every day. At least once, sometimes twice. Her letters
were warm and witty and contained quotations in Greek. I located
a friend of a friend who could translate them. She looked at me
rather oddly.

She went to a college near my home, three hours from Vassar. I
went home nearly every other weekend that year—my parents
couldn't understand why I should be homesick in my sophomore
year, when I hadn't shown any signs of it freshman year. Any
excuse to be where I could see her was good enough. My family
was particularly impressed by my sororal devotion when I came
home one weekend to see my younger sister play a walk-on part in
a high school play.

On weekends when there was no possible excuse for going home,
she came to see me at Vassar. If my friends thought it odd that I
had such a frequent female guest (and I am sure they did), they kept

it to themselves. My roommate obligingly found other quarters so that my friend could sleep in her bed. We talked late into the night. One Sunday night late in October or early November, she and I took a cab to the bus station in Poughkeepsie and I watched her board a bus for New York City. I felt so desolate at her leaving that I walked back to campus in a fog. I walked straight to the room of a friend renowned for her understanding ear and poured out my feelings. Sitting beside me on her bed, she said, rather matter-of-factly, "Sounds to me like you're in love." She'd put into words what I couldn't, or wouldn't, and it was as if the naming were permission-giving.

We first made love on Thanksgiving weekend (very quietly, in her bedroom in her parents' house) and remained lovers (with two years off for bad behavior) for the next 15 years. Loving her and being glad and proud of that love cost me the companionship of some Vassar classmates I had thought were my friends, but strengthened my friendship with the women who were truly my friends. Their support for me as I experienced the trials of my first love was wonderful. It was particularly wonderful in light of the fact that this was 1965, and there was little in their experience or education that would have led them to believe that lesbianism was anything

Vassar College, Sunset Lake *(photo © Anne MacKay)*

other than a perversion. These women simply knew that they loved me and that I needed them.

It wasn't easy being lesbian at Vassar in 1965-1968. There is a lot of pain in finding out that friends no longer consider you a suitable companion, in coming out to parents, in hiding one's affections. I knew no one else who was lesbian; I was afraid that being lesbian would result in my being thrown out of school, a fear not without grounds. I fought my own homophobia without knowing what it was, but it was great fun being in love. I remember going to my mail box in Main three times a day, hoping for letters from her, and finding at least one a day. I remember walking back with her from Main to Noyes on a snowy day. No one else was around and she suddenly took off her loafers (she never wore socks) and walked to Noyes circle barefoot. As we entered the line of trees, she looked back at her tracks in the snow and said, "There, let them wonder about that," and laughed and kissed me. I remember the time she took the train back to New York City and the conductor looked at her and said, "You have the look of a woman in love, but I guess I shouldn't say that, since you're coming from that girls' school."

ELLEN ANTHONY

What a waste of years and lives
and energy self-hatred is.

I am trying to understand why I feel so resistant to writing this bit of lesbian history as the equally complicated memory of the first lesbian/gay alumnae/i weekend lingers on. As Vassar has become coed, the magic of an all-female campus seems hard to conjure. That atmosphere of respect for women's minds, leadership, and creativity was something I took for granted until graduation, which is where this story could begin.

Instead, I'll start with Tim, my AIDS buddy, who will doubtless be gone by the time this is printed. For it is through my five years of volunteering with people who have AIDS that I have come to name and unpack my own bundle of shame about being lesbian, or perhaps about being born; such is the slippery nature of shame. What a waste of years and lives and energy self-hatred is. I see that so clearly with the men I've watched pass through the compression of retirement, reminiscing, and reconciling that AIDS can be. Such an eerie mixture of the horrific and wondrous: mothers who never show up, mothers who lobby Congress. Lovers the same.

I wanted so much to be famous after Vassar, actually *at* Vassar. So I played the bagpipes down the daisy chain and won awards for poetry. But maybe it is only when one knows death that the world's measure has less meaning and what has been waiting in one's deepest place comes forward. Not for approval, just for listening to. Well, if there is some blessing to the nastiness of AIDS and shame, then self-reckoning is one. It backs you down into yourself where there is no one left to love except you and so you begin to, or you die. Or, you begin to *and* you die.

In 1967 I was a sophomore on my way to get a hamburger with my best friend, Kate. We slouched our Saturday evening way up the rain-slick steps of Students under the tall white columns into the cozy joint with small round tables. We were jabbering on about blood in *Macbeth*, the notion of cultural bias from Intro to Anthro, and her latest plans to catch a man, when in strode a woman in a black cape with black leather boots, wild full hair over her shoulders. She could have been Lakey, but I had not yet seen *The Group*. I must have said, "Well" or "Wow" or "I'd like to get to know her, wouldn't you?" Aside from a few further references to Australopithecus and Iago, Kate didn't speak to me for several days after that.

When she finally stopped by my room to break silence, she stood there stiffly for a moment and then said, "I didn't know you were a lesbian." I was thrown against the back wall of my chest. I couldn't talk. I probably couldn't hear. I have no idea what either of us said after that. I only know I locked the door after she left and lay belly-down on my bed, staring out the heavy leaded windows into the night. What I saw was not an hallucination; it was a feeling that I recall as a scene. I was in a small brown boat waving goodbye to everyone I'd ever known who stayed on shore, on earth, which I had to leave now.

I didn't know I was a lesbian, but I accepted that she knew. It had occurred to me before, that I might be whatever that was, because since 12, since 16, I had loved women in my heart. They were the ones who moved me. But I didn't dare touch anyone or call myself that. Not until after college.

It was 1970. I marched on Washington to end the Vietnam War. I didn't march in the Christopher Street rally for gay rights. I wasn't ready. At Vassar there were the first purple signs, the essay "Woman-Identified Woman" by Rita Mae Brown attached to a student's door, announcements of consciousness-raising groups, petitions for this and that. I had returned, after a year of shy correspondence, to court my first love, a teacher. I knew some of those student pioneers only a year younger than I, but couldn't make contact or say I was there. My lover pulled down the shades of her apartment and we were never seen together. A solitary confinement of two that I felt must surely be wrong. So I fled. After two difficult months of passion and denial, I went to live with the Eskimaux, whose lifestyle would surely correct mine or freeze it. Teaching third grade in Newfoundland I ordered myself not to feel. And I wore out two pair of snowshoes with brooding.

In these 20 years since Vassar, I have shuttled between bold achievements and hesitant loves. My first documentary was about Karen Clark, an openly lesbian state representative. It won an award on Minnesota Public TV. Public liberation doesn't mean much, however, unless it derives from the private.

Last year in the middle of some confusing loving, nay, using all those messy feelings, I dared myself to play Joan of Arc in *The Lark*, the drama that launched my father's Broadway directing career. It all happened so fast I didn't have time for my usual loyalty to self-doubt. "What I am I will not denounce; what I have done I will not deny." Joan taught me to bust out of rules and categories, especially when they get in the way of inner convictions. She did not worry

Main Building *(photo by Cyd Emmons/Courtesy of Vassar College)*

about how messy it is to be a mystic in the world, a politician with a heart, a plucky idealist who must embrace her worst childhood fear—death by fire. She just did it.

Such energy is locked away in whatever parts of ourselves we fear or deny, waiting for just a little nod of attention without judgment. I have given up any territorial claim to shame or liberation. Here.

ANN NORTHROP

*I wasn't going to let anybody tell
me there was anything wrong with
this, because I had waited my entire
life, and now it was my turn.*

*Excerpts from a speech at the Lesbian and Gay Center, New York City,
December 11, 1990.*

I am certainly a child of the upper middle class suburbs. My
parents and their friends referred to one neighborhood they lived in
as the "upper gin belt"—a world of private schools and country
clubs. There were lessons all along about what was appropriate and
what wasn't.

I knew my feelings for my classmates were inappropriate. I was
in love with my gym teacher my senior year in high school. My
classmates started noticing that I spent a little too much time following this woman around. They would tease me and, boy, did I back
off. I said, "I must deny this. I must run away from this." As soon
as I could even begin to feel the feelings I had for other girls and for
women, I was absolutely horrified and terrified. Certainly confused,
certainly suicidal; lying awake at night inventorying the knife drawer
in the kitchen. I certainly never expected to achieve a moment of
happiness in life—never, ever. I was resigned to misery, to isolation,
to lying about myself every minute of every day. I thought that was
the way it had to be.

So there I was feeling miserable and doing the cliche thing of
burying myself in my career after college, because I was barely out

to myself at that point. And by the way, that's something I'm very ashamed of—well, not entirely ashamed—there were lesbians in my college time who were out and who had to really struggle and fight a lot of horrors because of the way they were treated there, and I was scared to be associated with them. I was really horrified by them, although they were my friends, and some still are my friends, but I kept them very much at arm's length. My escape vehicle at that point was television. Televisions were illegal in the dorms, but I had a small one, and I used to throw a blanket on it when I went on vacation. I was notorious for sitting around and watching a lot of television. In fact, in my senior year, I think I was averaging 80 hours a week—and there were days I didn't watch!

It was the classic business of just burying yourself, just going underground. I am somewhat horrified when I look back on it, but I understand it, too. And I'm so happy now and so grateful to have gotten where I've gotten that I don't have any bitterness about that really. I see it as what I had to go through. It's amazing to me that I've gone from there to here. I was completely closeted, did not talk to one single person on the face of the earth about my attraction to women, until I had a lover. Until I met a woman, who, after some months of us both being crazy about each other and both thinking the other was heterosexual, finally breaking through that and getting together in the most magnificent moment of my life. When Linda and I got together, *that* was the moment I could tell everybody. It was a black-and-white experience: one day not a word, never, to anyone; the next day, *everybody*. It's now 14 years later and we are still together. I was 28 years old when I first experienced love that was returned and fulfilled. It was a miracle to me. I felt like I was experiencing something that everyone else had been through, and I was very selfish about it. I wasn't going to let anybody tell me there was anything wrong with this, because I had waited my entire life, and now it was my turn. And that's what brought me out.

I went to college in 1966. At that point, I was in favor of bombing Hanoi off the face of the earth. You will be amused when I tell you who changed my mind. Harrison Salisbury of *The New York Times* gave a speech at Vassar College one night and read letters from servicemen in Vietnam about the atrocities they had committed, and it blew me away. I remember going back to the dorm and talking all night. I flipped, and became one of those people who are described as extremely dangerous: I was a convert. We had an all-

The Center Voice 7

A 'Lesbian American' Will Speak at Center In December

"From Debutante to Defendant: The Making of a Lesbian Activist" is Ann Northrop's story of her radicalization and the title of her presentation at December's Second Tuesdays at the Center series. The talk will begin at 8 p.m. on December 11.

An active member of ACT UP, Northrop has helped facilitate the group's Monday night meetings, demonstrated, and been arrested. She is also a member of Queer Nation and says she would most like to be remembered for her appearance on Channel 13 during Pride Weekend. Wearing a fashionably ripped Queer Nation T-shirt, she announced on the air, "Lesbians have always run everything."

Northrop, an alumna of Vassar College (B.A., 1970), was a print and broadcast journalist for 17 years (the first issue of *Ms.* magazine; CBS News). She now works with teenagers on issues related to homosexuality and AIDS in her capacity as an educator/trainer with the Hetrick-Martin Institute for Lesbian and Gay Youth in New York. ∎

Photo: © Bill Bytsura

Ann Northrop

college meeting to decide what to do: cancel classes, leaflet. I got up and said, "I'll talk against that," and I went up to the podium in the chapel in front of about 2,000 people and I said, "Look, this is nonsense. This is not how we're going to end the war. The only way to end the war is to get a machine gun and go to Washington and kill Melvin Laird [the Secretary of Defense]."

The Vietnam War was an enormous experience for me. I wasn't nearly as active as I am now on AIDS issues and lesbian and gay issues. I was peripheral at best, but I loved it. I loved getting out there and screaming and yelling, and that was the model for my getting into AIDS activism. I love the fact that I can go around to the high schools now and be part of the change. I talk to classes of kids and see kids sit up straighter and stand up straighter when they see me. Because they are lesbian and gay and they are feeling lousy about themselves and suddenly, here's someone who's telling them it's OK—they're happy and it's just overwhelming for them.

Achieving self-esteem has meant that I've dropped a lot of anger. What has happened is that I've come to an understanding that none

Strong House, with Lathrop in the background *(photo © Anne MacKay)*

of us can escape being homophobic. Every single person in the world is homophobic. If we are raised to be homophobic, we cannot escape it. I think that 99% of the world is simply ignorant, because they have not met us as human beings. I go out and do the training I do as a specific strategy. I confront what I think are the real gut issues, because I think no one ever talks about them, especially to kids. And that's why they hate and fear and name-call, because no one has ever had an honest conversation with them about how they feel and what they think. And it's amazing what you can achieve by giving kids permission to drop that language, to have an honest conversation with an actual, three-dimensional lesbian.

I think visibility is *the* bottom-line issue. I think until the world sees us wherever we are, whoever we are, whatever we are doing, in our full existence, we will not get as far as we need to go. I think that is the key: being visible.

BONITA ANN PALMER

I found that after going to bed with
men, my sex life was less interesting,
less exciting than the days when we
just sat in the front seat of the car
and petted.

From a tape made February 26, 1991.

I always had the sense of being different. In school, at the age of seven or eight, when the "cool" people get sorted out from the "not so cool," I remember being called a faggot and a queer. The words lezzie and dyke didn't surface until I was about 10 years old. But I was determined not to behave as girls were expected to behave—I felt defiant from an early age. I always got really good grades in school and excelled in everything. I was a student leader and knew even at age seven it was *not* OK to be a brain, and the older I got, the more "uncool" it became. I felt different—I never aspired to get married and have kids. I was ambitious. I had a sense that there was some reason I was on this earth and that I was to make a difference, to do something significant with my life.

My mother was in a very unhappy marriage. She wanted her daughters to have the college education that she didn't have and for us to be able to support ourselves in some respectable way and not have to depend upon a man. But she certainly didn't want me to turn out lesbian. From an early age I wanted to be a doctor. I never wanted to be a nurse, to be in a position of taking orders from men. The desire to have a career and be independent was really more a conscious part of my identity than the issue of whom I would end up with romantically or how I would define myself sexually.

I grew up on Long Island, New York, and graduated from Baldwin High School. My 13th year was a real crisis time. I ended up having a kind of mini-breakdown. I got increasingly angry at my mother; I couldn't figure out why she didn't divorce my father. I felt that nobody was listening to me, and I crawled into bed, pulled the covers over my head, and wouldn't go to school for several days. It was one of my first spiritual retreat experiences. I went totally inside and I said, "Stop the world, I want to get off."

What came out of that was that my parents sent me to my first psychiatrist. My mother had discovered some things I had written to a girlfriend who had rejected me that were clearly erotic. I had torn the note up into very little pieces, but my mother was the type of woman who felt it was perfectly her right to come into my room and snoop around. So I ended up seeing this Freudian doctor for several months. One of the first things he wanted to do was examine my genitals, and he started to educate me about heterosexual sex. I know now that he was really trying to change me, but he was the first adult I could talk to. I started dating boys when I was 14—I think I was sexually curious. My boyfriends were good friends and I could share a lot with them.

Much of my involvement with girls was through Girl Scouts. I loved camping. That was my time to get away. When I was 14, I became a counselor's aide. It was obvious to me that a lot of the counselors I hung out with were lesbian.

That same year at camp, I got this really intense crush on one of the counselors. I remember how it felt—this intense energy—it was amazing. I knew something was going on; the heartbreak was intense, yet it didn't really affect how I behaved when I got back to Baldwin High.

I won a New York State Regent's scholarship and discovered when looking in a directory of New York schools that Vassar was in New York. I fell in love with the school when I went to see the campus. Something came over me and I really wanted to go to Vassar. But I hesitated because it was an all-women's college and I thought it was not going to have a very good social life. I agonized over this and went back to the psychiatrist I had seen many years before. I asked him, first of all, what he thought was wrong with me when I was 13. (In my mind there had to be a mental illness in order to go to a psychiatrist, and previously he had said "personality disorder" or something.) So he said to me, "Well, there's really nothing wrong with you. You're just an extremely intelligent young woman." That was why I was having problems?! He then tried vehemently to dissuade me from going to Vassar, although again, the "L" word was not directly mentioned. He also tried to talk me into marrying my boyfriend, who was 19, a freshman at Brooklyn College. Well, I knew *that* was a dumb idea. It's clear to me now that he was trying to save me from lesbianism.

My going to Vassar was one of the best decisions I ever made in my life. I had this growing sense of myself as a strong woman, somebody who was different, someone who was going to make my own way. I was a little intimidated at first. I lived in Josselyn, which at that time was heavily loaded with socialites, and this was my first experience of the upper class. It was a kind of culture shock, again, a feeling of being "not cool."

I took a heavy course load and was afraid my first semester about my grades, but ended up on the dean's list! At that time at Vassar, the social life consisted of going to mixers with all these really bright young men from West Point and Yale, etc. I was dating a man from my hometown who was 22 or 23. I had lost my virginity, on purpose, the summer before. I got him drunk one night and managed to have sex in the front seat of his car. I was definitely the aggressor. I was just so sick of making this a big deal over whether or not I was going to have intercourse with a man—that this was the definition of my worth as a female. After doing that, good Catholic boy that he was, he freaked out and treated me like I was a witch or something and rejected me. Then he got drafted to go to Vietnam. He turned around, came up to Vassar, and asked me to marry him. It was high drama.

This is how out of touch I was with myself. I had intentionally started sleeping around with men—it was as much rebellion as anything else. But I found that after going to bed with men, my sex life was *less* interesting, less exciting than the days when we just sat in the front seat of the car and petted. Having intercourse was just not terribly attractive. But I had a series of relationships with men while I was at Vassar. I did a lot of chasing after men and wondering why it wasn't working. In part, I think this was in reaction to my being raped the summer after my freshman year, and this delayed my coming out.

Much to my regret, I never did have a love affair with a woman while I was at Vassar, although I did have crushes. In sophomore year I changed dorms to Cushing where I could have a single room and be where the artists were—people who were less social and more into politics and studying. I felt more at home. Eventually I started to meet lesbians at Cushing. Freshman year, there had been some seniors in my dorm who were lesbians and were very, very bright. None of them seemed to get in trouble, I think because they stood up to the administration and were top students. I remember there was a woman my freshman year who was rumored to have left school because she'd been caught with another woman. In those days, apparently, you'd get called in to see Mrs. Drouilhet—the Drou they called her, the warden, who was in charge of housing. She'd been there forever and ever. Women would get called into her office and confronted with the evidence, and some would drop out of school.

But more of an issue then was not having men in the dorms. Freshman women were only allowed to take four weekends off campus, and they had to know where you were going. You could have men in your room, but the hours were limited and everybody knew who came and went—you couldn't even go off campus without signing in and out.

In my sophomore year, I decided to go to Williams for the second semester because I was worried about going to medical school. This was prior to affirmative action and all the medical schools were still heavily male. Some schools only had two percent women.

I really loved my academic life at Vassar. It was very creative, very stimulating, very supportive, and very non-competitive. There was a high standard, and the understanding was that, of course, we were going to reach for our best, for excellence. I wondered how I would do in a very competitive male environment. So in 1968 I decided to go on the first exchange to Williams and that's when my eyes started opening about the degrees of sexism that existed in the Ivy Leagues. People at Williams were debating whether women should *be* at Williams. We were either going to ruin their academic reputation or we'd be so good we'd break the curve on which they were graded. The women from Vassar were treated either as potential dates or academic threats.

The summer before, I had started smoking grass. I was smart enough to know not to drop psychedelics, although Timothy Leary had come to Vassar preaching, "Tune in, turn on, drop out," and some people did. But I felt I was missing out on the revolution. I did OK in my classes, decided to go to medical school, and survived Williams by getting involved in the theater. That's when I started meeting gay people.

I went back to Vassar as a junior and was very glad to be there. I dug into my classes with vehemence and really focused on getting good grades for medical school.

But 1969 was quite an eventful year. That fall, consciousness-raising started happening on campus and there were meetings in Cushing. We would sit on the floor and talk about our lives in new ways. I remember Kate Millett in those meetings. She was working on her doctorate at Columbia at that time, and her dissertation, of course, ended up as *Sexual Politics*. Rita Mae Brown was also there—she was organizing in New York—that was when the Lavender Menace raised its head within N.O.W. for the first time. She had been working with N.O.W. and they broke off and started Red Stockings and Radical Lesbians. My feminist awakening was very much in the context of a largely lesbian-defined community. There

Cushing House *(photo © Anne MacKay)*

were many gay women in Cushing and my feeling was that I belonged in those groups. I continued to be involved with men sexually, and my senior year, a man lived with me in my one room at Cushing. No one ever confronted me about it, though it must have been apparent to the faculty living there as well as the students.

Vassar is a unique environment, it has a wonderful history of affirming women's intelligence, women's integrity, and full and equal rights for women in society. I would hope that tradition lives on, even as the institution educates men alongside women.

I would encourage the gay and lesbian students at Vassar to value this heritage. I think that the issues around feminism and gay and lesbian liberation are very linked, that the denigration of the feminine and of women is at the heart of the homophobic backlash. I would just say to students: Have the courage to be who you are and find support and community with other students. Learn about your heritage and culture. Work toward a more fully accepting society and acknowledgment of the unique gifts and unique roles we have to play as gay and lesbian people.

Editor's Note: *Bonita Ann Palmer did go to medical school. She did come out as a lesbian and 11 years ago received a religious call. She has worked in various ways within the Episcopal Church to do outreach to the gay and lesbian community and has lobbied on behalf of Integrity for effective lesbian visibility for the Council of Women's Ministries. In 1988 she was seated on the Council as the first open lesbian member. She was also one of the founders of the California Association of Lesbian Physicians, now a national network associated with the American Association of Physicians for Human Rights.*

NAME WITHHELD

Marriage never seemed like a

good idea . . .

I do not have any stories of delight or misery; however, I am agreeable to being counted. I graduated in 1971. My partner and I have been together since 1984.

It seems to me that my choices in life have not been as difficult for me as similar choices have been for many other women. It has always seemed clear to me that qualities of character were more important than gender. I appreciate the social consequences of *not* choosing wifehood and motherhood, but the institution of marriage being what it is, motherhood being what it is, men being how they are, and society being how it is, all outweigh those consequences.

I was involved with men, almost exclusively, until about eight years ago. Marriage never seemed like a good idea, though. Not marrying, and settling down with a woman, has not been traumatic. My work suits me well (I am a lawyer for the federal government); I have time for my personal interests; and generally, life is good.

ANN E. MENASCHE

*I remember very clearly reading an
article in the* Vassar Miscellany
News *about lesbianism.*

I had no awareness of being gay before college. Though I had crushes on girls as well as boys, I interpreted them differently. My crushes on girls were merely admiration. I had heard that Socrates was homosexual, but I had no conscious awareness of lesbians. In high school, I was a misfit and had problems making friends. I was terribly lonely and blamed myself for all my difficulties. During my junior year, I made a conscious effort to make my dress and behavior conform to that expected of a teenage girl in the hopes of finally getting a boyfriend. When it worked, my self-esteem was still so low that I had a hard time believing a boy would find me attractive. Yet, on my first date, I laid it on the line—I didn't want children, I wanted my career, and if I ever got married, it would have to be 50/50 in the house. This was pre-feminist 1967. I was instinctively a rebel.

During my first two years at Vassar, I continued to be socially ostracized. During my spare time, I mostly hung around with my boyfriend. At the same time, I became involved in progressive politics on campus and in the mid-Hudson Valley SDS (Students for a Democratic Society), the anti-Vietnam War movement, and an underground newspaper called *The Gargoyle*, that was shockingly male-dominated by today's standards. I soon found that I was more outspoken around men than most of the young women I knew, and less (hetero)sexually liberated. However, I still felt that there was something wrong with me.

Though I was strongly infatuated with my boyfriend and it was an exciting experience becoming political radicals together, I was also becoming increasingly disillusioned with the relationship. He was pressuring me to agree to marry him after graduation, which I didn't appreciate. I finally agreed, just to shut him up. I also found myself always having to fight for my dignity. Like many men, he was at times physically violent. Frequently, he would talk down to me as well, yet expect me to take care of him and put his needs before my own. I was surprised to experience loneliness even when I was with him. I felt ambivalent about him; yet at the same time, because of my isolation, I was very dependent on him.

Though there were strong, articulate women I admired at Vassar, and I made some acquaintances, I still had no close friends. Women, for the most part, continued not to like me because I was different. I found, as I had in high school, that there was a lot of competitiveness among the women about who had the best boyfriend or who was the most cool or liberated, and not a lot of real communicating or bonding.

Toward the end of my second year at Vassar, things started to change. I remember very clearly reading an article in the *Vassar Miscellany News* about lesbianism. I remember reading that the potential to love other women was in all of us. At that moment, I knew deep down that this was true for me.

Around the same time, feminism started happening. All the things I had always felt were finally being affirmed from the outside. Women started being more honest with each other, acknowledging that being the all-American girl wasn't all it was cracked up to be. One night, I talked to a woman until 2 A.M., leaving my boyfriend impatiently waiting in my dorm room. She confessed that she was miserable in high school dating all those football players and being a cheerleader. She assured me that I hadn't missed a thing. It was a revelation. Maybe there was nothing wrong with me after all. I began to feel better about myself. I also started making friends.

And then I met a student at a nearby community college. My brain, the most important sexual organ in my view, now had a slot for lesbian, knew such a thing existed, and so I fell head over heels in love. This was the beginning of a very slow coming-out process for me. I was extremely frightened as well as exhilarated by my feelings and hesitated to identify them for what they were. And she was more male-identified and lesbophobic than I was. So nothing physical happened, except we used to hug a lot. She broke my heart numerous times. I used to cry my eyes out and my boyfriend would comfort me. What a fool!

What made it really hard was I had no lesbian friends to talk to, though I had begun to know who the other lesbians were. Once, I slipped a note to a lesbian I admired on campus, asking if she would talk to me about my feelings. I received no response. I did have some brief conversations with a couple of bisexual-identified women at school, but it didn't help much.

Though I was struggling with these lesbian feelings within me, I was fairly open about it. I submitted love poems I had written to my creative writing class [see page 101]. It was scary, but the reaction wasn't too terrible, probably because I was still writing heterosexual poems. In another class, I experienced a much more serious put-down and was even given a poor grade for writing a feminist critique of D. H. Lawrence's *The Fox*. I attended probably the first lesbian/gay organizing meeting at Vassar during my senior year. I talked a little to my straight friends about my feelings. And on one occasion, I attended a lesbian support group in Poughkeepsie. I didn't say a word there. I wasn't sure I belonged. I had a boyfriend, after all. And I had never even had sex with a woman. How could I be a real lesbian?

After I graduated from Vassar in 1972, I moved to San Francisco to go to law school. This was a fortuitous move. I was 3,000 miles away from my boyfriend, and San Francisco was already becoming a hotbed of lesbian and gay cultures. In the early to mid-'70s, women were coming out all over the place and beginning to sing about it and write about it. It was an incredibly exciting time. It was relatively easy to become a lesbian then. It has probably never been easier before or since. Actually, I think in the last decade, it has begun to get harder again.

In law school, I made my first lesbian friend, a woman who confirmed my feelings ("Being a lesbian is in your head and in your heart, Ann") and took me under her wing. By 1975, I was ready to take the leap. I became involved with my first woman lover. Soon afterward, I officially dumped the boyfriend who was still waiting for me back East. That final step was actually the hardest—harder than sleeping with a woman or wearing a gay button to law school. I felt like I had cut all ties with legitimacy and normality as a woman, putting myself officially "beyond the pale." But I was lucky. I had a lot of support for my transition, and an unusually understanding family and a burgeoning sense of my own self-worth that I had nurtured at Vassar. But without feminism, without a lesbian/gay movement, without that wonderful article in the *Vassar Miscellany News*, without knowing that lesbians existed as real people, it would probably never have happened.

My lesbianism was and is both a political choice growing out of my radical feminism, and an emotional preference for the depth, equality, and mutuality possible between two women, a preference that was brought to fruition during favorable times. I don't believe that people are born with any particular sexuality. Rather, I believe any woman has the potential to love other women, and if the social environment permits it, choose to create a woman-centered life, though rebels like myself may be more likely to do so. I also believe that if you don't fit with the heterosexual script, as many women don't, conformity can exact a heavy toll. The women's movement rescued me from a lot of potential unhappiness. Though the price society makes you pay for violating its strictures can be severe, I think it is worth it.

I am now living in a committed partnership with a wonderful woman. I continue to be very politically active, as I have been since college, including working for feminist and lesbian/gay causes. Three years ago, I helped form a lesbian-feminist organization in the Bay Area called "Lesbian Uprising." We now put out a newsletter that reaches over 300 lesbians and organize community events. This group has become my extended family of friends. It is through the group that I met my present lover.

What I have to say to women Vassar graduates who find themselves struggling with the issues I did is this: Be patient with yourself. It is never easy being different. Find lesbians to connect with and talk to. Don't let anyone convince you that your feelings aren't genuine or that you can't be a real lesbian, or that there is something wrong with you. Being a lesbian is a healthy, life-affirming choice. Read lots of books. Work for women's liberation. And learn to love yourself, because if you don't love yourself, you'll find it extremely difficult to resist society's message and open your heart and soul to loving other women.

IF THE BUDS

If the buds
      like butterflies
Spread their wings
      of palest green
        again
I will yearn for you
Remembering
How we walked through Central Park
Your long black hair
      beating
        against your breast
And shared secrets
      like bread

Now, hidden away
      like a small, brown
        rabbit
Shivering in the muddy
      tunnels of earth
His body laid upon you
      like cement
And you, like a weed,
      pushing yourself
Through the pavement
      And into the sunlight.

      —Ann E. Menasche
      Written at Vassar College
      in 1972

73

CARLA DUKE

After all, these things spread like

wildfire in a women's college.

An actual article in the *Vassar Quarterly* (Winter 1990) about being a lesbian! I never thought I'd see the day!

I graduated from Vassar in 1973. To the best of my knowledge, I was one of the first openly lesbian students at Vassar who was not expelled for her "condition."

I entered Vassar in 1967. I had first heard of Vassar because of Edna St. Vincent Millay, and I had read *The Group* by Mary McCarthy. I realized I was a lesbian at 15, and by the time I arrived at Vassar at the age of 17, I was trying to consider my lesbianism in a positive light, although I had not yet met another lesbian. I proceeded to come out to all my friends and acquaintances during my first year. The reactions I got were quite varied: some never spoke to me again; some acted like they didn't care, but were a little uncomfortable; others made a point of making a lot of sexual innuendos and jokes, and somebody put me on a pornographic mailing list.

In the spring I became involved with someone who lived in a different dorm (I was in Lathrop), and we had trouble finding a place to be alone on campus, since we both lived in double rooms. She had an English teacher who said, "Well, if you need to be alone, why don't you use my office in Avery?" Her office was up in the front tower and had a bed that was like a couch. So we would go and use her office. I don't know if she knew what went on, but it was wonderful to have a place to go. This was my first real relationship. We were sexual together and I loved it. For the first time in my life I felt good about being a lesbian.

At the end of that year, she went away and decided she wouldn't return to Vassar. I was heartbroken and we wrote to each other all summer. When my mother went through my wastebasket on a pretext, and found some crumpled unfinished letters, they made me go to a Freudian psychiatrist, who said that anything I dreamt of that stuck up in the air was a penis. It was very invasive and ugly and the only reason I did it was that they threatened to call my friend's parents if I didn't.

As a freshman and sophomore, I was involved in the campus movement to give students more power over the rules governing their non-academic life by changing the college governance. I worked on the underground campus newspaper, *The Student Onion*. (In those days there were only the officially supported *Vassar Miscellany News* and *The Onion*.) In 1968 I was president of the student delegation to the Minnewaska conference to change the governance.

In 1968–69, when I was a sophomore, I transferred to Cushing and fell in love with someone. In January, my mother and stepfather told me they had been steaming open my mail during the vacation and realized that I was still a lesbian. Since I wouldn't go back to the therapist, they disowned me, and I went to live with my real father, who saved my life. My mother and stepfather also threatened to expose me to the director of financial aid (I was on a full-tuition scholarship) and the dean of residence. So I went to both offices, explained that such a letter was coming and asked what the policy was and what I needed to do to stay in school. I still remember the Drou telling me she was sorry, but the policy was I could stay in school only if I sought psychiatric help; that maybe when the college went coed this rule could be dispensed with. After all, these things spread like wildfire in a women's college. So once a week for the rest of the school year I went to see the study counselor, who was less understanding but much less offensive than the Freudian psychiatrist my mother and stepfather had sent me to.

I returned for my junior year fired up with feminism. I scheduled a meeting and over 100 women came. We suddenly had a feminist movement on campus. Several of us started a group. I went to a NOW conference in New York City and met my first acknowledged lesbian, Rita Mae Brown. Soon thereafter, several other women in the group decided to come out, and we invited Rita Mae to come up and give a poetry reading and talk to us. She brought Pat Minnardi, Cynthia Funk, March Hoffman, Kate Millett, and others, and a strong connection was born. We visited back and forth on weekends. We read first drafts of the "Woman-Identified Woman" article. We were assigned positions during the lesbian invasion of a NOW conference, traveled to Boston and Yale for discussions and planning. The net effect on the campus was a full-blown radical lesbian group of five to ten women that seemed to have sprung from the forehead of Athena. We staged a feminist protest at one of the college mixers: one woman cut off her long hair; I danced around in a coed skirt and sweater, my hands tied with a pearl necklace, and then went on stage and ripped both off as I made a statement. Of course, we complained bitterly about the way the few men who were on campus were taking over and being catered to. And so much more. It was exciting and, for me, it was like coming home to a home I never knew existed: the lesbian community. My grades suffered and it was suggested I leave for a year.

So I spent the following year in New York City and then in Washington, at first with Rita. Then I became disillusioned with her and I pulled away as she was getting involved with what later became the Furies in Washington, DC.

In 1971–72, I came back to Poughkeepsie with my lover. We lived off-campus. I did my thesis on the writings of Gertrude Stein and got involved with the Poughkeepsie and New Paltz women's and lesbian community. Jackie Saint James was being his flaming, flashy self on campus. A Vassar Gay Student Union formed, but the lesbian presence was greatly reduced. My radical lesbian perspective was considered eccentric and unique at best. I remember making recommendations on campus living that would help keep a coed campus a comfortable place for a radical feminist lesbian. People's mouths were wide open.

What a shame now to look back and wish someone could have told me that Emily Dickinson and Willa Cather were lesbians. When I did my thesis, there was still controversy over whether Gertrude Stein was really a lesbian.

74

REMI ST. CLOUD

I projected a consciously and openly

gay persona.

To describe my sexuality when I was a Vassar undergrad as "not so hidden" would be regarded by my schoolmates, I suspect, as a colossal understatement. I entered with the very first freshman class to include males, in 1970, at which time I projected a consciously and openly gay persona to dormmates and classmates, faculty and administration, the school, and, I suppose, the world. Though I attended two other schools in the interim, I graduated along with my original fellows in '74. During this period and briefly afterward, I went by the name Jackie Saint James. This was as much or more in keeping with my high social and political visibility as a controversial gay personality as with my academic major: drama.

My long ago conviction to be gay and proud (how archaic that phrase rings today; almost biblical-sounding to my jaundiced '90s Manhattan ear) yielded a most wondrous and wholly unexpected dividend: more than a few closeted women and men, most of them struggling and many cruelly tormented, sought me out as a safe harbor. Thus I found many confidantes, several lifelong friends, and a lover of four years.

Bear in mind that when I came onto the scene as a non-apologetic homosexual, I experienced some negative response as well. Some of it was direct and visceral, while some, particularly that which emanated from the college administration, was subtle and intangible. In the middle of my freshman year I found myself on paper-thin ice in a legal matter due to an unfounded allegation against me by the parent of a local high school student I was tutoring under the auspices of a college-sponsored program. If this all sounds a little seedy and silly, what followed was worse. A college administrator attempted to sweep the matter under the carpet, explaining that I in no way represented the college, that I might soon not be enrolled in the college, that I was virtually on my own in this matter. Meanwhile, I had decided to run for, and was elected, class president. This made all the difference in the world. No one could now allege that I was not "representative." And I learned an important lesson: the Vassar administration would respect an individual's right to be different; they would not officially sanction, or more importantly,

HAVING FUN IN THE SEVENTIES

Jackie St. James & friends at Pizzatown *(photo © Terry de Roy Gruber '76)*

defend that right unless to do otherwise posed a threat to the school itself.

I served as president of the class of '74 from the spring of my freshman year through the end of my sophomore year, at which point I left the college for England. I returned in the winter of my junior year and was elected senior class president, and simultaneously won the appointment as Editor-in-Chief of the 1974 *Vassarion* from the retiring editorial board. I delivered the only student address at my commencement exercise, and from 1971 through 1975 was variously covered by the *New York Times*, *Newsweek*, *Esquire*, the *Poughkeepsie Journal*, the news departments of two national networks, and three or four local stations, and more. I cite all of this only to establish one point: the college president, vice president for Student Affairs, chair of the Board of Trustees, virtually everyone but "the Drou" (Elizabeth Moffat Drouilhet, dean of residence, who in my observation, bowed to no one), protected me, consulted me, cosseted me only when they saw that I and, in its local infancy, gay pride, were going to be a part of Vassar's history, like it or not.

One last note: my view is that the percentage of Vassar students involved in same-sex relationships in the early '70s was far nearer 30 than 10.

NAME WITHHELD

*We weren't lovers, but we told each
other that if one of us were a man,
we would have been.*

I am one of the 10 percent who graduated from Vassar.

I didn't come out until eight years after I graduated. Mine was the class of 1974, the one that stirred up some controversy with an *Esquire* magazine article that portrayed Vassar as a very gay and risqué place. They had interviewed our class president, Jackie Weiss, aka Jackie St. James, and others.

Freshman year I became close with a woman in Strong House. Strong was one of the three dorms that remained all-women that first year of coeducation at Vassar. My friend and I were nearly inseparable. We would sit in the stairwells talking till all hours of the night. We'd have our meals together, take late-night walks, climb the trees in the quad, and sneak into the chapel to listen to organ practice. We dressed alike and looked similar enough so people would mix us up. I learned to answer to her name.

We weren't lovers, but we told each other that if one of us were a man, we would have been. We would touch hands sometimes. It was very innocent, but made my roommate uneasy. She told us we were sick and asked us not to do it.

Sometimes we speculated about whether some of the upper-class women in Strong were lesbians, but we never turned that conversation inward.

Sophomore year, we had single rooms across the hall from each other in a different dorm. My friend drifted from me that fall, befriending others. I was confused and hurt, but unable to put into words that my heart had been broken.

After that, my confusion remained unexplored, unnamed.

I got in with a very straight group of people. I remember whispers and snickers about one lesbian couple in the dorm. Most people seemed preoccupied with the heterosexual dream, which wasn't easy to actualize in those early days of coeducation. I remained on the periphery.

I've been back to Vassar many times since I graduated. Last summer I finally felt comfortable enough within myself to be out at reunion. My life partner came with me and we had a fine time. My classmates were very accepting.

Our examination of the student center bulletin boards informed us of the existence of gay and lesbian groups on campus, but we got the impression that they have a hard fight. For that matter, the topic of date rape was in the news, an indication that women are still far from equal, even at Vassar.

We, gay and lesbian people, need to bring our existence into the open and demand our human rights and protections. Unfortunately, that's often difficult in practice. I remain ambiguous on my job. The rumors have circulated, but I haven't been confronted, nor have I come forward.

Two years ago, I finally told my parents I'm a lesbian. They responded with sadness, fear, condemnation, and bitter words. That sent me into therapy, which has been a very positive step. It's true, we all come to self-understanding at different points in our lives. To be gay is to miss out on some of society's prescribed rites of passage. Maybe someday that will change.

75

DEIDRE MCCALLA

It was the source of a fair amount of

controversy on campus as it

contained two scenes where the

female leads kiss.

My mother rarely forwards copies of the *Vassar Quarterly* to me. She knows that for the most part I couldn't care less. But for some reason, bless her heart, she sent me the Winter '90 issue and I'm glad she did. After reading the article on "Breaking the Silence," for the first time in years I felt connected to our Alma Mater.

My story "At Nineteen" is in an anthology called *The Coming Out Stories*, edited by Julia Penelope and Susan Wolf, and republished a few years ago by Crossing Press as *The Original Coming Out Stories*. It chronicles my coming out at Vassar and some of the circumstances surrounding the formation of the first Gay Students Union on campus (at least we believe it was the first) in 1972.

In retrospect, the early '70s were interesting times to be lesbian or gay at Vassar. Being gay had a certain bit of mainstream chic; it was the heyday of the David Bowie glitter rock scene, which was extremely popular at the time. Since the school was newly coed, a lot of media attention focussed on the suspect sexuality of the male students, which the lesbians always found amusing because we knew there were many more dykes on campus than there were faggots.

I was a theater major and for my senior thesis I directed a lesbian play, Susan Miller's *Confessions of a Female Disorder*. I had to fight the Drama Department tooth and nail to get it approved and it was the source of a fair amount of controversy on campus as it contained two scenes where the female leads kiss. Nonetheless, it played three sold-out performances and the department grudgingly gave me an A on the project. At the time I did not consider myself very "out"; looking back, I realize that I should have been wearing one of those T-shirts that say, "NOBODY KNOWS I'M GAY."

Editor's note: *Deidre McCalla is one of our star performers. She has recorded two albums for Olivia Records:* With a Little Luck *and* Don't Doubt It.

DAVID PITTMAN

The conservative backlash began,
with the rugby team in the
vanguard. An era in which it felt
safe to be gay at Vassar was
drawing to a close.

The period from 1974 to 1978 was a good time to be an openly gay student at Vassar. Some credit for this may be owed to certain members of the preceding classes whose flamboyant behavior assaulted the limits of acceptability. The *Esquire* article in which they were featured, shortly before I arrived for freshman orientation, would indirectly contribute to the conservative backlash that began in the late '70s. But in the interim, I found a relatively safe place in which to come out. For a few glorious years it was cool to be gay at Vassar.

As a high school senior I considered going to Vassar for the usual reasons. I also like the idea of being the sixth member of my family to attend Vassar, thus carrying on a 100-year-old tradition. But I chose Vassar primarily because it seemed like a place where I could grow personally, which meant coming to grips with my sexuality.

I arrived without any idea how to go about coming out, but during my first semester I got started. For me, coming out was synonymous with becoming part of the gay community. This was a network (you wouldn't call it a group) of students who occupied various and shifting positions on the spectrum from straight to gay. They were a remarkable bunch, both individually and collectively. The class of '74 may have laid some of the groundwork, but it was the members of the succeeding classes who created the atmosphere in which I grew from a fearful sissy boy into a proud gay man.

At the end of my sophomore year I made two important decisions. One was to accept the position of chairperson of the Gay People's Alliance. Having one's name printed in the student handbook as the leader of the GPA was about as out as one could be. I was concerned about my ability to lead the group, and as it turned out my fears were well-founded. We got off to a reasonably good start, but fizzled out after the first semester. It was not an illustrious chapter in the history of the GPA.

The other decision was to move to the Terrace Apartments with three friends. One of them took a leave of absence before the fall semester started and the other two did likewise before the semester was over, so I had five different housemates by the end of the year. Together we created a space in which the sense of safety and belonging that I had already felt at Vassar was intensified. Our TA was like a little gay ghetto, the Greenwich Village or Castro of Vassar.

Though I did not especially like all my housemates at first, I came to love each of them in time. I was finally able to let go of a crush I had on one of them that had been an obstacle to our friendship, and with another found it was possible to have a friendship with a straight man. During the spring semester I was surprised to find how much our third roommate and I had in common. The first two were the carefree, happy-go-lucky ones while we were more inclined to be serious or moody. Although I am only in touch with one of them now, I continue to think of them all as my friends.

There was little overt homophobia then, but the administration ensured that this would not last. I do not know whether fears that Vassar would develop a reputation for being a gay school first arose before or after the publication of the infamous *Esquire* article. I do know that a new director of admissions was hired, that his goals were to enlarge the applicant pool and achieve a 50-50 gender ratio, and that it was deemed necessary to marginalize students who were outspoken women and/or openly gay in order to assure sexist and homophobic high school students that Vassar was not just for sissies. I learned of this policy through the publication of an admission brochure that highlighted the rugby team and the presence of male students in prominent positions on campus, and some of us protested. Meetings were held between representatives of student organizations, myself included, and members of the administration. We had some success in convincing them that we liked Vassar just the way it was.

We may have won the battle, but the war was already lost. By senior year the classes recruited under those homophobic policies already made up half the student body. There were no fewer gays in the class of '80 than there had been in earlier classes, but there were plenty of young Republicans, as well. The conservative backlash began, with the rugby team in the vanguard. An era in which it felt safe to be gay at Vassar was drawing to a close.

I visited the campus several times during the fall of 1979 and spring of 1980, while my boyfriend—now my spouse—was a senior. It saddened me to find that the spirit of my generation, the feeling of personal freedom that had attracted me to Vassar six years earlier, no longer dominated the campus. This sadness has since been overshadowed by a greater one caused by the deaths of several members of that generation, including two of my former housemates, Rick and David.

I feel fortunate to have been a student at Vassar at that special time, to have known that remarkable bunch, and to be able to share this story.

Name Withheld*

. . . she always felt that kissing was
something boys and girls did.

I fell in love with my roommate freshman year, and there's no doubt it changed *my* life.

When I came to Vassar I left Neil behind. Actually, it took a while to realize that Neil was not the one for me. He was my high school boyfriend. The only one I ever had. I came to Vassar and was absolutely miserable. I missed Neil, my family, my security, and I was intimidated by this wonderful and famous school I had chosen. I think I cried most days, and the loneliness was unbearable. At one point, I even applied for—and was granted—a leave of absence to attend the University of Buffalo, where Neil was. But then at Vassar, a friend's roommate moved out and I moved in. We became fast friends, quite inseparable. Vassar started looking pretty good after all, and luckily I never went to UB!

Soon, I found myself wanting to be more than just her friend, but I didn't quite know how to go about it. Being a true Vassar girl, I decided to research the matter. I can't quite believe this now, but I remember very distinctly going out fishing that summer with my

---

*I'm very sorry not to have my name used here, but my partner in the story would not give her permission. She doesn't feel, and I agree, that her identity could be hidden.

father. While he trolled for "muskies," I sat in the boat and read *Lesbian Nation*, *Lesbian/Woman* and *Sappho Was A Right-On Woman*. I also told Neil it was *over*.

That autumn, I went back to Vassar determined to put my research into action. However, fear of rejection and a very deep-seated embarrassment made me revise my plans. I remember very distinctly that at the beginning of October, I decided there was no way—I was just too shy. But things were happening. Little things. Sophomore year, she and I had separate rooms. We'd be studying in her room or in mine and she'd say something like, "Could you throw me that book?" I'd respond, "What'll you give me?" To which she would invariably reply, "A hug and a kiss." Maybe there was hope after all. Then there were those evenings in the "Libe" where I'd try to concentrate on psychology and not on the fact that she and I were playing an innocent game of footsie under the table. Well, pretty soon I started threatening to collect all those hugs and kisses that were stacking up and earning interest! Then, one night, it happened.

It was 2 A.M., October 14. I had just turned off my light and hopped into my little bed. Do you believe we actually were able to sleep on those tiny straw-filled mattresses? I heard a knock at my door. It was *her*! I invited her in and reached to turn on the light, but she said, "No, don't bother." And she hadn't even done any research like I had! We sat on the bed and had one of those very memorable conversations college sophomores have about Life—the world, the future, our pasts, hopes, dreams. I can't remember a single thing we said. Then, since it was October in Poughkeepsie and it was by now 4:30 A.M., and those damn clanking heaters weren't turned on yet, we got cold. So I wrapped my robe around her, then the sheet, then the blanket, and then, well we were both under the covers, facing the wrong way, as I remember. Somehow, that made it seem safer! We slept, wrapped in each other's arms.

The next day I went to my English class, dazed and exhausted, but filled with excitement and expectation. Too tired to pay attention to the teacher, I doodled—flowers, sunshine, birds, and the words "What a Beautiful Day Is Today." Actually, I think it rained most of the day. Did I care?

Two nights later, she came to my room again and somehow, over the next few weeks, we became lovers. It took a while, because there were so many barriers. Well, maybe we could take our tops off. But that's all. OK, next night maybe a little more. But not our underwear. Are college sophomores today as innocent as we were? Kissing remained a barrier. Maybe her lack of research became a handicap here, because she always felt that kissing was something boys and girls did. Not two woman—at least not too often. Not at first.

She and I stayed together six years. I like to include our freshman year when we were "just" roommates. When she went to Washington for part of our junior year, I thought I wouldn't survive. But I did, and so did we. The breakup came two years after Vassar, when she was in law school and I was at the same university getting my master's. She met a man and decided it was time to get back to the straight and narrow path. After a brief and very difficult time, we were able to become friends again and have remained so to this day.

I love the fact that I came out, and that it happened at Vassar the way it did. I have never regretted being a lesbian; in fact, it's one of the things I treasure the most. I know that we have a lot of the same problems that straight people have. And I guess we have some that are unique. But we also have a community that I have found to be supportive, accepting, and in many instances, progressive.

I have always had trouble trying to understand the fears that some people have about their sexual identity. For me, it has just seemed easier to be open about who I am. It takes too much energy to keep pulling the closet door shut. I don't often find it necessary to come out to people. I just talk about my life and who I spend time with and where I go. People just catch on. And if there's any confusion, I don't hesitate to clear it up.

I think Vassar helped me develop a real sense of pride in who I am. Growing up and becoming a mature and productive adult is hard for just about anyone. But I feel strongly that my Vassar background has given me an advantage in that regard. I'm currently in school again, at the ripe old age of 35, studying to become a doctor of chiropractic. At first I was shocked and appalled at the sexism, racism, and homophobia I encountered at school, especially from the younger students. I remember Vassar as a place where, if you disagreed with someone, at least their opinions were well-thought-out and demonstrated a certain degree of flexibility. Maybe we were lucky or maybe it was just the times.

Now, I often feel like I'm in an intellectual wasteland, and a very conservative one at that. I'm currently in a bit of a struggle with the administration at my school. Several of us are trying to start an organization of lesbian and gay students and friends. Unfortunately, the powers that be seem to think we will be the downfall of chiropractic if word leaks out that there are queers in the profession.

Oh well, it just makes me more eager than ever to forge ahead. Thank you, Vassar, for helping me find the courage.

DANIEL AIBEL

. . . he is still my best friend and
the man of my dreams.

When I arrived at Vassar, everyone seemed to be open and comfortable with their sexuality but me. The "cool" people seemed to swirl about in a dance of sexual openness and experimentation. They lived in Terrace Apartments or Town Houses (I hadn't even figured out where these were yet), and they descended on campus only when necessary to assert their social mastery. They were always smarter, funnier, better looking, and more accomplished. Most freshmen strove wildly to establish places in some branch of this glittering elite by claiming some new and shocking frontier. On my hallway, there were transvestites, leather biker types, teenyboppers, groovy organic types, and even a devil worshiper.

In contrast, I was a quiet, bookish, private person. My sexual orientation was entirely hypothetical (indeed, I thought it likely that no one would ever be sexually interested in me). While I thought I might be gay, I seemed to have nothing in common with other gay people. I had no interest in being shocking, weird, or even fashionable. I spent most of my time alone; hoping, yet terrified, that someone would notice me.

By the end of that first year, I felt totally unwanted at Vassar, and I transferred to a school with a more traditional atmosphere.

But I didn't fit in there either, and I struggled to understand why I was different from other people at school.

In the summer of my junior year, I began my return to the Vassar fold. I had a chance meeting with someone I had known at Vassar. Most of her friends had graduated the year before and had been part of the cool elite. Outside of Vassar's special atmosphere, however, they no longer seemed so distant and superior. They had been forced to adjust to a world which did not offer Vassar's protection for individual differences. I found that we were in a common struggle for our identities.

Although I decided to focus on strong friendships to avoid dealing with my lack of sexual success, this decision was turned on its head when I met David. He had been the object of one of my hopeless freshman crushes, and he still made my heart flutter. I pursued his friendship, but found that mere friendship was not enough. Suffice it to say that our courtship remains a swirl of excitement and magic in my mind. And that excitement and magic have never died. David and I are still together. Although we have had problems at times, he is still my best friend and the man of my dreams. I look forward to growing old with him. After many years of "living in sin," we celebrated a marriage ceremony in 1990.

In order to be close to David, I returned to Vassar my senior year. It was a different place from freshman year. The days of the cool elite had passed. Being weird and different was no longer in style. Those who tried to express their inner differences with external signs such as thrift shop clothing, leather jackets or hair dyed purple were no longer campus leaders. Instead, they were regarded by others with suspicion and disrespect.

There was a sense of sadness in Vassar's lesbian and gay community. When graduates came to visit, we would sit around talking of the wild days that had passed. It was clear that the days of glory were over. Personally, I had mixed feelings. While I understood the sadness, I knew that none of the people I now had as friends, including my lover David, would have noticed me in the wild days. I felt grateful to those who, through wild expression, had forced the entire Vassar community to confront its diversity, and had forced lesbian and gay students to find common bonds. But I also felt that there was now a place for me in a calmer lesbian and gay community.

I saw the calmer days partly as a sign of growth within the lesbian and gay community; we were no longer a special elite or a world apart from the rest of Vassar. While it might have seemed that the community was less diverse in that we no longer sought to stand out as different from other people, a new diversity came from an acceptance of ordinary lesbian and gay people who were in different circles. Individually, each of us was oriented toward resources and social lives outside of the lesbian and gay community. Because we came from different social circles, there was not much cohesiveness between us and we were not a concerted social force. We were each fighting separate battles for acceptance in our respective circles. Ultimately, of course, the object was the same. Thus, when we did come together, for example for the 1979 March on Washington, we found we had more in common than we would have admitted.

In 1980, I read the first short articles flatly reporting strange cancers in a few gay men. I remember discussing these articles with David and others in our circle and hearing vague rumors that something bigger was involved. To a large degree, I believe that the AIDS epidemic has drawn people from my years away from our separate circles and into greater unity. We have been forced to share not only our oppression, but also our grief. The common threat has provided the impetus for us to declare our identities in order to find allies in our struggles. We have been forced to look at ourselves for leadership as an older generation has been passing before its time. As the barriers against us have been diminishing, we have started to blaze trails of respectability.

For me, the real story is about how I have grown through my love for David and how that love has grown despite the odds against us. I wish I could communicate the rewards possible to people who are unsure about taking risks and following their hearts.

GEORGIE TIRRE

When those love feelings came, and I
felt them toward a woman, I was
first just in love. Then I just
wanted to die.

My name is Georgie Tirre. I am a lesbian. I attended Vassar in 1975 and 1976. If I just talked about the me in '75–'76, well, that would be pretty scary.

Today I live in Hercules, California, a suburb of San Francisco. I am very lesbian-identified, work in a law firm, and am "out" to select professional peers. I am finishing up my last year of law school at Golden Gate University, a place where I have never been in the closet. In short, today I am finding it much easier to love myself for who I am. But it has been a very long and painful road.

I am also an alcoholic in recovery for the last year. I say that because I think my addictive personality helped me cope with my homophobia by numbing out, using a variety of substances. Today it is my responsibility to show up, homophobia and all.

Now, going back to Vassar seems a bit more bearable. Those were very painful years. But I don't blame Vassar. Vassar was just like most of the country, out of it when it came to the gay and lesbian community.

I think if I could offer any advice to someone experiencing the pain of isolation I felt, it would be, just don't give up. Life does get better.

At Vassar I was a self-contained, ambitious thing, who had a hard time feeling any feelings, and feelings of love were the hardest of all to acknowledge.

When those love feelings came, and I felt them toward a woman, I was first just in love. Then I just wanted to die.

I told the student I loved her, was rejected, and fell apart. I wouldn't wish that rejection, coupled with isolation, on my worst enemy.

There were people with whom I shared my pain and was comforted. But the struggle with my own sexual identity and self-acceptance took many more years. In fact, it is ongoing.

LISA MALACHOWSKY

For me, it was a kind of rebirth and
I felt like a new world was being
presented to me.

In 1976, my sister wrote to give me directions to her house in Brooklyn, New York. I was going to visit her for the weekend. Along with the letter was a photo of a woman I had never seen before. I wondered why she sent me this photograph and who was this woman? I learned on page three of her letter. My sister had decided that I needed to know some things about her life before I got to her house. One of those things was that she was a lesbian.

Lesbian. What does that word mean to someone who is 15 years old? Does it connote something good or something bad? I had no idea, but I knew that my sister would never be something bad. She was someone I always looked up to. She was someone I wanted to be like. So if she was a lesbian, it must not be a bad thing. The stage was set and my questioning began.

Although my sister was a big influence on my childhood, she wasn't the only influence. Many things made me feel that I was not like most of the girls I grew up with. I wasn't interested in boys when they were. I was heavily into playing sports and being outdoors all of the time. My father was a more important parent figure to me, because I perceived what he did for our family as having more value than what my mother contributed. I know now this sounds rather innocent, but these differences in my socialization pulled me away from traditional girl-like behavior.

I started expressing my sexuality late in my teens. I was already at Vassar. I was 17 before I actually lost my virginity to a man. I hate that phrase, because I knew exactly what I was doing. I wanted to want what I was doing. But somehow the physical feelings and experiences that followed did not match what my heart was telling me. I continued to date this man, who was also a Vassar student, for two and a half years. During most of the time we dated, I never felt completely comfortable with our relationship. But there were times when we were very much in love and attracted to each other. I had even thought that we would get married. So for the first time in my life, I thought that I was getting "normal." There were also other times when I felt very empty, very alone. He cared very much for me, but told me often that I could become very unapproachable. I didn't know where this was coming from within me. We had numerous conversations about our sexuality and individuality and came to the conclusion that something was going on with both of us. He felt that he had to experiment with other relationships— other expressions of his sexuality. I didn't know what I wanted, but I was curious about what he was suggesting.

So all of this finally led us to some serious talk about what we wanted from each other. And we came to the conclusion that both of us were trying to live out lives we really couldn't be happy with. I was disappointed that my first real relationship had failed, but at least we weren't hurting each other by breaking it off before we grew too attached. I was free to choose what I wanted to do next. But what did I want?

I was gradually coming to a realization that would not be easy to live with. I had already been through some very rough times trying to cope with and accept a sister coming out of the closet to family. You would think that would have made it easier to deal with for me. Nothing could be further from the truth. I remembered enduring a day during which my mother said to me, very emotionally, "If I ever find out that both of my daughters are gay, I'll just kill myself!"

How can a person who loves her mother do something she knows will bring her grief? I was beginning to get very unsettled and confused.

With all of this going on inside my head, I spent the last three months of my sophomore year on the verge of something. I was not communicating well with anyone and I began putting distance between myself and each of my friends who had a boyfriend. I hadn't expressed any homosexuality openly at this point and wasn't feeling attracted to anyone I knew. I confided in the one friend I really trusted and found some solace, but no satisfaction. This was something I knew I had to work through and resolve on my own.

One day, an unexpected letter came from a high school friend. She was interested in seeing Vassar, because she was considering it in her list of colleges to apply to. I quickly wrote back and told her that she was welcome to come and stay with me to get a taste of the Vassar educational experience. It took several weeks to work out the details.

She arrived. We spent time walking around the campus, looking at the facilities she was interested in, and I even took her to a Philosophy class with me. At the end of a fairly hectic day, we lounged around in my room. Something was troubling her and even though I hadn't spent much time with her in the past few years, I knew that it was something which would need the right atmosphere to come out. Unfortunately, we got off on a tangent about religion and my relationship with my boyfriend and never got to the right plane of thought. She went home and decided not to come to Vassar.

But then she began writing me regularly and finally invited me to spend March break in Rochester, New York, with her. She had decided to attend the University of Rochester instead of Vassar. I accepted the invitation.

We did many ordinary things during the day and finally a subject came up that I wasn't prepared for. She wanted us to go to a bar where we could dance a little and play some pool. She wanted to know if it would bother me that it was a woman's bar. At this point in my life, I had only known one lesbian fairly well: my sister. I was curious about what went on in lesbian bars, so I told her it was not a problem. She also asked me if it would bother me if her lover met us there. I said, "No, not at all." My mind began to formulate questions. Had I seen any tendencies in my friend as we were growing up? Had she seen something in me? What was going on really? I couldn't gather my thoughts into a coherent set of facts. I needed a set of truths to understand why this scene was being played.

So we played pool and I watched all of the women there dancing—really having fun. My friend bought me drinks (many more than I could handle). I observed her lover getting aggravated. I was the center of my friend's attention and I was getting drunk. Finally, I asked if we could go back to her room and I apologized to her lover for not being able to stay. She went her way, visibly upset but trying to be polite, and we started back to my friend's dorm room. The air was cold and by the time we got there, I was almost sober again.

After getting her room set up for the two of us to sleep, we were both fully awake. I decided to be brave and ask what was going on with her. She explained that she had met her lover and instantly knew that she was attracted to her. She began to relate her story of falling in love for the first time with a woman. But I could hear something else in her voice that had nothing to do with her present lover. Her words weren't forthright, but she was coming on to me. I let go of my inhibitions and kissed her. The response was what I expected: sweet reciprocation. We spent the night renewing our friendship and exploring each other's bodies. This was what was bothering her during her visit with me at Vassar. She was attracted to me but unsure of what to do about it. The next day, I wrote in my journal:

> How does one describe feelings and emotions and ecstasy never felt before? I don't know, but what I do know is that making love to her was like something indescribable. THAT WAS TRULY MAKING LOVE the way it was meant to feel.

Unfortunately, I only had one more day to spend with her before going back to Vassar and classes. We couldn't keep our eyes and hands off each other. For me, it was a kind of rebirth and I felt like a new world was being presented to me.

After the glow of passion and newness sank in, I realized that I had allowed myself to do a very selfish thing. I had begun a relationship with someone who was already involved with someone else. This was very complicated. Distance separated us and other ties bound my new lover. So this relationship became very painful and very quickly disintegrated.

But my eyes were now firmly, widely open. I returned to Vassar with renewed hope. I immediately sought out other lesbians and organizations for gay students. I needed to connect with others like me and learn that I was not the only one.

It took a while to find my sense of community and it wasn't what I had expected. I felt very much like an outsider in the organizations full of strong-willed and opinionated women. I didn't know what to think or say most of the time. I felt intimidated by all of them who had gone through this much earlier in their lives and seemed to have no sympathy for me. Only one person reached out to me individually and that was all I needed. I needed a confidante. I needed someone to respect. I found that one person. She was a good friend and still is. She understood that I wasn't the kind of person who could be forced to form opinions and voice them just by being in the company of similar spirits. I had always been a person who needed one or two good friends to feel in equilibrium and she was starting to bring me back to the balance point.

During the rest of my Vassar residence, I hovered on the edge of the gay community, but felt that was where I needed to be. I still had and needed my straight friends, but was starting to feel less dependent on them. I was also working part-time off-campus and began to meet new people who were in no way affiliated with Vassar. Through one of these people, I met my present lover, who I have been with now for seven and a half years across two states.

I guess you could say that I didn't really come out at Vassar, but I did come out while I was studying there. Overall, I would say that Vassar neither inhibited nor intensified my process of coming out. It was an environment that acted like a passive filter for my experiences. My path was chosen and charted by me with guidance from individuals I met along the way.

83

COLIN D. O'CONNELL

It was quite safe to be a gay couple

on the Vassar campus at

that time.

I knew that I was bisexual, most probably homosexual, when I came to freshman orientation at the Vassar farm in the beginning of my freshman year in 1978. After the fun, festivities, and camaraderie, I met a fellow freshman who lived in my dorm and had my first comprehensive experience with a member of the same sex before freshman year started. You know, it was really nice to be able to follow my feelings and express myself with a classmate at a school where I had hoped I could be a "liberal" liberal arts student. I knew I had made the right choice because I understood that it would be safe to be an openly gay student.

Prior to Vassar, I had spent three years at Choate-Rosemary Hall, where I was very restricted in my personal expression and individual freedom. (I was not yet considered an adult.) At Vassar, I was able to indulge myself in sometimes outrageous expressions of individuality. I acted out quite a bit! In retrospect, my idea of having a gas was to party a lot and then dress in drag and go to a big campus party. I really had a devil-may-care attitude toward anyone who was offended by my cross-dressing. I was aiming to shock people, to amuse people, and just to act out a fantasy of dressing up as a woman. Since I had a fear of venturing out to Greenwich Village in New York with other gay and lesbian friends, where I might also dress in drag, I seized the opportunity at Vassar. But then again, quite a few men on campus—gay, bisexual, and straight—dressed in drag for a screening of *The Rocky Horror Picture Show* in the fall of 1978. So, certain men at Vassar also enjoyed being outrageous by dressing in drag. One chum went through a full day of classes dressed in a kilt, a cute white blouse, a Fair Isle sweater, a red hair band, sensible hose, and clogs. Not many people were fazed!

One good thing was that the Gay People's Alliance had been founded and was active. The GPA had regular meetings, activities, and always threw the best dance on campus. I went to the GPA dance at Vassar this year, the Homo Hop, since I now live in Cornwall, New York, with my lover and it was nothing less than phenomenal. I was enthralled by what appeared to be a thriving gay community at Vassar. When I was a student, there was a bit of antagonism between certain factions of the lesbian membership and the gay male membership of the GPA, which resulted in the founding of a separate lesbian group, the Feminist Union. It's too bad that not everyone was aware of the concept of "principles before personalities," but I guess for many members of the GPA at that time it was brand new to be an active, vocal part of a gay community. And they chose to be very vocal.

I entered into a gay relationship at Vassar which was to last three years. We were a very visible male couple on campus. I can't recall any cases where we were jeered, bothered, or rejected as a couple by the students, faculty, or staff. It was quite safe to be a gay couple on the Vassar campus at that time. Certain cliques of the gay community would always congregate in certain areas or rooms at ACDC for meals. The relationship I shared at Vassar was sometimes quite stormy, but straight friends would come up to us and say that seeing us together despite the turbulence gave them a lot of hope. They would say things like, "God, if you two can stay together in the midst of everything, it really gives me hope for my relationship."

It was quite apparent that certain members of the faculty and administration were homosexual. I was very glad that they were there, because it allowed me to see adults around me who were living proof that you could come to terms with your sexuality, and they served as examples to younger homosexuals. Having older homosexuals around us made me feel less isolated and helped me realize that my sexual orientation was but a part of the entire being I manifested.

Vassar Campus *(photo © Anne MacKay)*

84

Susan Williams

We kissed for what felt like 45

minutes . . .

I was born in New York, raised in Queens, and went to Stuyvesant High School. I was sexually active with men from the age of 16. I had no inkling of my deep sensual feelings for women until the day I was first kissed by a woman sophomore year at Vassar.

In high school, I was involved with the co-captain of the men's wrestling team. We considered ourselves "normal" and the other world of "faggots" and "lesbos" was not. My friends and I picked on and tormented these "other" people. I was obviously quite aware that gay people existed, but had been socialized very traditionally— that is, not to accept them. I knew I was not one of them, though I have since realized that little experiences can come back to haunt you later. For instance, looking back at my time in high school I realize I had a crush on the girlfriend of the other co-captain of the wrestling team. I staged a pretend wrestling match with her once and remember feeling exhilarated by her touch. It wasn't until my second year at Vassar that this memory surfaced.

I arrived at Vassar in September 1980. As people formed friendships, it started becoming evident who the gay men and lesbians on campus were. There were individuals who insisted on taunting and teasing the gay people, but I had changed and now found this behavior unacceptable.

My freshman year was a time to explore relationships and sex with men. My high school boyfriend and I had broken up prior to college, but when I heard he was going to Vassar, too, I said to myself, "Great, now we'll have a chance to get back together, marry, and live happily ever after." I was naive, to say the least. Yet desperation set in and I accepted any time he would allow me with him. I knew he was sleeping with other women. It drove me crazy, so I started sleeping with other men. I look back on this time and see it as a learning experience, a progression toward who I am now. These initial college experiences prompted me to start keeping a journal. It was sophomore year and I was living in a Town House with four other women.

The date is October 14, 1981. I'm studying with my best friend in her bedroom. The door is closed and we're bored, so we start to tickle each other. We're on her bed and she suddenly pins my shoulders down. I feel a rush of confusion and awkwardness. I'm uncomfortable with what I'm feeling and say, "I've got to go to the bathroom." She stares at me and calmly says, "Not until you kiss me." So here I am, being propositioned by my closest friend—the girl I spend time talking about boys with—and I kiss her. I'll never forget that kiss, and I know she won't either. It was the most delicious, the softest, the meltiest kiss that I'd ever felt. We kissed for what felt like 45 minutes but in actuality was only five minutes. The kiss ended as suddenly as it began; she got up from the bed and said, "OK, now you can go to the bathroom." I tried to get up, but my knees weakened and I stumbled as I went to the bathroom. I came back and said, "Oh my God, I think my life just turned 180 degrees." We talked about what had occurred between us. She admitted that she had felt bisexual since high school, but had never acted on her feelings for women until this kiss. That night we went to bed together. I was really scared, yet it felt like the most normal thing in my life. I knew what to do; I knew how to please her. I simply asked myself, "What would I like?" It was the most wonderful experience. As strange as my life had turned that night, I didn't wake up the next day and say, "I'm a lesbian now, everything's OK." Instead, I felt crazy.

We were involved for about a month. I even came out to my mother during this first relationship. Things finally ended for us when she started dating men again. Though this ending was painful, I felt free to explore my newfound sexuality.

About two weeks after we got involved I began attending Gay People's Alliance (GPA) meetings. I was attempting to sort out my identity, trying to decide if it was only her I wanted or women in general. I started going to women's bars with the lesbians in the GPA. I remember the first time I finally got the courage to walk into a women's bar; I felt like I had come home. I was exhilarated and found all the women so uniquely beautiful. I knew I had found my world, my people.

The first person I told about my new sexuality was a man I had been in love with. Our relationship as friends was still close. I felt safe with him. I remember telling him that I thought I was bisexual or gay (I didn't use the word lesbian yet). He was very supportive and said I had a lot of guts. This first coming out experience was very validating.

Gradually my relationships with women became news on campus. Certainly the most exciting event that happened to me at Vassar was the publication of the November 11, 1982, issue of *Rolling Stone* magazine. I was really in love with my newfound sexuality, and I had offered to be the contact to the woman writing an article on "America's Gay Women." I felt exhilarated by women and the gay community, and it felt fun being "deviant." I also got together with Beth, the woman with me in the *Rolling Stone* photo, and had my first long-term lesbian relationship. When the *Rolling Stone* article was put up on the bulletin board in Main building without the photo, I quickly proceeded to Dixie Sheridan's office and said, "Dixie, I'd like the photo to be up, too." So the next week the article came down and the photo went up. I went back to Dixie's office and said, "You know, I'd like both the article and the photos up together." So instead of being displayed one week, I made it for three weeks. By now it was no secret; everyone on campus knew I was a lesbian. As I made this transition from straight to lesbian, the vibes on campus changed. Some people were so scared of me, they would avoid touching my shoulder as they walked by me. In general, women seemed scared of me and men were intrigued. Since so many women I knew and cared about were totally flipped out, I gravitated to the gay community, which took me in. They didn't say, "Ugh, you were once straight." Instead they welcomed me. I found a place of support.

After the article came out, a lot of people whom I had called my friends wouldn't speak to me. I became invisible to the man I had been involved with for years. He would not talk to me, he would not acknowledge me. I was obviously no longer a person worth communicating with. Yet the most significant loss for me at that time was a past roommate. We had been really close friends. One day I went to her room to tell her that this woman and I had become lovers. She seemed quite uncomfortable with this news. The next day I found her door locked. I banged on it and confronted her about her behavior. I told her how hurt I was. Eventually we had a long talk about what being a lesbian meant to me. It *didn't* mean that I desired all women. I told her that I loved her, that she was my friend, but that I wasn't sexually interested in her—that our relationship was like being straight and having male friends. Though her initial reaction to my lesbianism was very difficult, times together eventually got better.

The GPA had numerous events and sponsored the best campus dances. Looking back, Vassar seemed quite a safe place to be gay. Unfortunately, the semester I went to England there was violence on campus from a group of individuals who called themselves "surf-Nazis." They harassed lesbians, gay men, Jews, and black people. The administration called campus-wide meetings concerning the racist and homophobic acts that had occurred. By the time I came back the tension had lessened.

In 1983, a small group of women wanted a student organization that was specifically lesbian-identified. We formed the Lesbian Feminist League (LFL). We had to convince the student body that there was a need for this kind of group; that the GPA didn't take care of all lesbian needs. I am still proud of being one of the founding members of the LFL, as well as one of a larger group of people who petitioned to get "sexual orientation" into Vassar's non-discrimination clause. We wanted to make sure that someone applying to Vassar could freely include in their entrance essay that they were lesbian or gay and not fear rejection simply because of that fact.

After Vassar I went to England and lived there for four and a half years. I found that I had to adapt to what the English thought lesbians were supposed to look like—conformity was the message that was put out. I identified as a lesbian though I kept any feelings I had for men hidden. It wasn't until I came back to the United States and moved to San Francisco that I realized that all lesbians don't have to look the same or be poor. And it certainly doesn't mean that you can't talk about fantasies involving men.

I identify as a lesbian because I find it easiest. Lesbian visibility is important to me in our society. It seems to me that the term "bisexual" is amorphous and that bisexuals haven't evolved into a strong community yet. For now I feel very comfortable with being a lesbian and calling myself one. I like the sound of the word and have certainly identified myself that way since Vassar.

LESLIE F. KLINE

. . . sexual abuse at 13, attempted

rape at 19 . . .

Your excellent article in the winter 1990 *Vassar Quarterly* reminds me yet again of my own immaturity and narrow-mindedness while at Vassar.

I recall my discomfort at the thought of the lesbian couple who lived in Jewett (my dorm for three and a half years). Their room was physically invaded by Vassar men who were threatened by their choice of lifestyle. I recall my own unease as a staff member of *Womanspeak* when I was in the company of another staff member I knew to be a lesbian. I was uncomfortable when we were working together alone. Would she make a sexual advance? What would I do? I respected her intelligence and commitment to the creative work in which we were engaged. However, I was not as confident in my own sexuality as I thought she was in hers. The threat proved to be unfounded. When I remember how I felt in this woman's presence and see how relaxed I am now with any woman, straight or lesbian, I am ashamed of my immaturity.

My cousin announced he was gay when I was still in high school, and my mother told me it would be much harder for her to adjust to my being a lesbian than to my brother being gay. Somehow it would reflect badly upon her as an imperfect mother for raising a daughter insufficiently feminine.

Dear friends I met during law school have educated me to a greater level of acceptance of their lesbianism and bisexuality.

My own experiences of sexual abuse at 13, attempted rape at 19, and virginity to date make me wonder, as I endure this lack of a love partner, whether I am bisexual. But I am sure that any bisexuality in me would be simply a result of turning to women I know to be compassionate and gentle, because I am unable to find a compassionate and gentle male partner.

JANA RICH

*One of the most valuable things I
learned at Vassar was a tolerance
for ambiguity—that things are
not as simple as gay/straight,
black/white, etc.*

I came from a small town of 4,000 people in Maine, about an hour northwest of Portland. Vassar was an incredibly broadening experience for me. I was very involved at Vassar, serving as a student fellow and house intern in Jewett, chair of the Student Committee on Admission, on the Major's Committee for both Psychology and Women's Studies and, ultimately, president of the class of 1989.

The following are brief excerpts from poetry I wrote during the spring break of '88. I had been involved in my first lesbian relationship (and first sexual relationship for that matter) with a straight woman, a senior at Vassar. I see this piece as a place of great struggle for me, making real my feelings for this woman while, at the same time, trying to understand that my feelings were not exactly reciprocated.

I think one of the most valuable things I learned at Vassar was a tolerance for ambiguity—that things are not as simple as gay/straight, black/white, etc.

> you caress my face lightly
> lightly grace the contours of
> my nose

my cheeks
my eyelashes
and they respond
to your touch
and try to give you pleasure in their own right
a back rub that was not to remain one-sided
my hand shakes
from nicotine
and zinfandel
i've never cried this much in my life
it's as fundamental a part of my existence nowadays
as eating
sleeping

as i watch smoke rise up to cover my face
i picture you
the only light playing on your face
is from the waves of light from the tv
you gently blow smoke past your nose and eyebrows
those peaked eyebrows
the professor said in my composition class one day
about how you remember a lover not through this whole
    elaborate scene
but by one physical characteristic in them that has the
    power
to evoke deep feeling
and i told you, only pretending to be embarrassed,
that it was your eyebrows

i know your lines so well
do you sense the warmth of my eyes
touching you
barely gracing the outline of your face
with a gentleness
that my forefinger would do
if you'd let it?

so much reminds me of you
you pervade my day
my mind dances from one image to another

and all of them are you
every time i light a cigarette
you are vividly present
"drink, smoke, cut"
playful
smiles
unabashedly, unreservedly happy

VALARIE WALKER

*It felt like somebody had just torn
my heart out and mailed it
somewhere and I had no return
address.*

Excerpts from a tape made on May 14, 1991.

I didn't know I was gay before Vassar—not at all. I had known
a lot of boys. I was raped when I was 16 by somebody I didn't
know. And before that I had been oblivious to sexuality. My mother
had given us great capacity for love, but I had never caught on to
the sex part. I had a boyfriend, but we didn't have sex until I was
18, just fooling around. I broke up with him my first semester at
Vassar. I lived in Strong. I remember calling my mother when I
found out, saying, "Oh my God, I'm in an all-girls dorm. I'm going
to have no social life. It's horrible. And my roommate is from Maine,
and there are only two black people in Maine and they're a tourist
attraction!"

Then I met this woman who was plagued with a lot of problems
about being away from her family. I'm very much a mother figure.
All I have to see is a need and I'm there. So we became really good
friends and I knew something different was going on in her head. I
remember she came into my room one morning and got into my
bed while I was getting ready to go to English class, and said,
"Valarie, there's something I need to tell you." "What?" "I can't say
it." "Is it something that—[the only out lesbian in the dorm that I
knew] would know more about than me?" "Yes." So finally she

wrote on a little piece of paper that she was in love with me. I said, "OK, stay here, I have to go to class—we need to talk." So I went to class and spent the entire time thinking about her. And then I went back and was so afraid I just said, "Look, I love you so much and your friendship is important to me, but you know, I don't feel this way about you. [I was so homophobic!] I understand that being with me is too painful, and you need some time and space . . ." Well, two days after that we were sleeping together.

We were together for two weeks and then it was spring break. We wrote and called each other. It felt like somebody had just torn my heart out and mailed it somewhere and I had no return address. It was awful. Then one day I got a call from her and she was crying and hysterical and couldn't talk. She said, "My father found out. He went into my room, he looked in my journal." He had beaten her severely and fractured her jaw, which was why it was so hard for her to talk, and said he was going to kill her. Then he took her out of Vassar.

I had never gone to the Lesbian Feminist League when I was a freshman, but some of them knew me from just living in the dorm. I didn't know until much later that they had had a meeting and were trying to decide what they could do to help my friend—if they had enough funding to get her out of her family situation and support her through Vassar. It made me cry that these women who didn't know me cared about the pain I was feeling and her pain and were ready to go to bat for someone they didn't know at all!

I had told my mother about her, but not about sleeping with her. My mother said she could understand it happening once—after all, being in an all-female environment for the first time, the boundaries of friendship were bound to get a little blurry. But if it happened more than once, then I would be sick. And that was fine, because, after all, I knew I was *not* a lesbian. Also, even though I was in love with her, sexually it wasn't all there for me.

I had support during this time from a good friend who had been going through her own stuff. We were both in hell, our first relationships were over and she thought she was going to be alone the rest of her life. We did sleep together once and it was very sweet, but it didn't affect our friendship and that was good. But we went home that summer and started courting each other through letters.

When we came back to school, we were both student fellows. We had all these children running around and going, "Waaah," and all we wanted was to be together! But we couldn't really say that to each other. So we made an agreement. Since we were really good friends, and she was the person I liked most and I was the person she liked most, we would use each other to explore our sexuality. Since we weren't in love with each other, there wouldn't be any heartache. It was good, because we were able to be honest with each other and find out about ourselves and our sexuality. And we were out of control! We were crazy kids—it was great. But then, of course, emotions started to get involved and we decided that we were getting too close, that we needed to try making out with other people. We needed to assert that we weren't crazy about each other. At this point I still didn't think I was a lesbian, but it was so much fun and I loved her so much there seemed no reason *not* to be with a woman. Later, after we broke up, our circle of friends broadened, but she has remained one of my closest friends.

At the end of my junior year I took a semester off and worked in the city over the summer to help pay my tuition. I had thought that being gay was just something that happened to me when I was at Vassar. But I got involved with a woman in New York City and when I got back to Vassar it was like: Not only am I a lesbian, but

Vassar College Main Building *(photo by S. Math/Courtesy of Vassar College)*

I am a *dyke*! And I am the best dyke you ever did meet. It was all coming from myself and I was so excited. I came out to a lot of people and didn't get one bad reaction.

I am also an activist. At Vassar I was always screaming and yelling, and I helped get a rapist kicked off campus through rage and personal testimony. I am now a member of ACT UP and ACT BLACK. I'd like to say to any other Afro-American woman of color who is out there and struggling with her sexuality and feels there are no role models, there *are* other black women out there who will appreciate you for everything you are, so go for it!

In my last year, another black lesbian and I did a forum called "Homosexuality in the Black Community." We held it in one of the smaller parlors and it was crowded! There were black people from Poughkeepsie who came and we sat and talked about what was going on and worked through a lot of stuff. She and I were both respected for being outspoken and we wouldn't let silence prevail. So that opened up a lot of dialogue where before there was none. And there are now many more black lesbians at Vassar and others who have had lesbian experiences. And that's such a positive thing. It's so much easier to be gay now at Vassar than when I was there. And I'm glad.

Karin Cook

. . . there is a wholeness that I
feel in being with women. I
wouldn't have known I was missing
it before . . .

Excerpts from a tape made May 8, 1991.

I have very fond memories of my time at Vassar. I was critical of Vassar the entire time I was there, but I think it was because I had a sense of the potential at all levels. So while it may have seemed that I was angry and disappointed, I really loved my time there. I grew so much and was able to challenge Vassar because of Vassar. Because of what I was learning academically about multiculturalism and feminism, I could turn around and look at the college structures and say, "Wait a minute, this isn't being reflected here and I'm being taught it should be. Let's do something about this!"

For me, being a lesbian is inextricably linked to activism. I can't see them as separate. I worked with Stop Rape Now, a group that formed initially in response to an incident of rape at Vassar and grew to become an educating advocacy force on campus. All of the structures at Vassar now relating to issues of sexual violence are there because of the work that Stop Rape Now did. It was an incredible group of people and I found my strength in women during that time. I will never forget the people in that group.

I almost didn't go to Vassar because of its history as a women's college. Isn't that unbelievable? And this became the reason I stayed.

I didn't know I was gay before college—far from it! I went to high school in Greenlawn, Long Island, New York. I had very serious relationships with men and, other than a few close female friends, I had not spent time with groups of women. Vassar was my first exposure to being with lots of women. When I look back, I know I was in love with women, though not identifying that way. I used to ride horses and there was a woman who also rode after whom I modeled my life. We had similar interests and I applied to all the colleges she applied to. I had her pictures all over my room. My first day at Vassar, one woman who was an activist was pointed out to me as being a lesbian and I noticed her; I definitely noticed her!

I came to Vassar in a very heterosexual context. I had been the cover model winner for *Young Miss* magazine. I love thinking that the magazine picked this well-rounded "all-American" girl, and I'm a dyke! Serves them right! I did print work with Ford Models for three years. I still stumble across those damn teen romance novels with me on the covers. This is what is in my closet, but is an important thing for me to remember because I've changed so much, I can't pretend that it was *not* part of my experience. Freshman year I was involved with men. I've had some bad experiences, but I've also had some very good ones with men. But I always felt that something was missing, not with them in the relationship, but I always felt as if I was supposed to be somewhere else. And often I literally *was* supposed to be somewhere else, at a gathering or meeting. My time felt very split to me.

I signed up for Women's Studies my freshman year. I wasn't sure at registration that I wanted it; I was scared to death because I think I knew what it meant for me. But I took the course and it really opened up a whole new world. Being a lesbian happened academically and politically before I made the personal connections. I took an AIDS class and I remember thinking that all the straight people sat on one side of the room and all the gay people sat on the other. I went and sat with the gay people about halfway through the semester. It was such a big deal to me, but I don't think anyone else even noticed.

In my sophomore year I worked politically with other women and had my first relationship with a woman. I was very fearful, because it was so different for me and I was coming from such a heterosexual context. I blew it because I had so much internalized homophobia and was too caught up in the idea of "what did it mean to be a lesbian?" I was struggling with this idea of identity and wasn't dealing with the relationship. I didn't do very well by that woman, but we're still good friends and I think she forgives me. My next relationship was with a man. I remember sitting in the Retreat once with him and looking at a painting of men with a woman in the background and I made a comment about her. He stopped me and said, "You know, you never, ever have a thing to say about men. You never comment on men." I turned red. I was so embarrassed and felt really exposed. He was a man I was very close with (we had been friends before being involved romantically), and he was telling me something I hadn't even been telling myself.

In my senior year I fell in love with a woman I knew from my Feminist Theory and Black Feminism classes. I had been crazy about her from the first day I saw her in September, but we didn't get together until February—it was a long crush, on my part anyway. We worked together politically during the Main takeover, which was a 36-hour occupation of the administrative offices. We were protesting the lack of institutional commitment to multiculturalism. At Vassar it existed in word; we wanted to see it exist in deed.

There are many complex issues to contend with in an interracial relationship, and to be lesbian in addition—it wasn't easy. Just being in love wasn't enough. It was work. What we were able to make work at Vassar became more and more difficult to achieve after we graduated and no longer had that environment in common.

I really disagree with what many people were saying at the LAGA conference (April '91), that everything is just fine on campus in terms of harassment. This was not my experience and certainly not the experience of some people who are still there. I think there's a lot of backlash going on because of the increased visibility. I think there are many people who feel very threatened by the gay presence.

I was a Mug manager my last year at Vassar [*Matthew's Mug, a student bar in the basement of Main Building, is named after the brewer, Matthew Vassar, who founded Vassar College*] and I hired an all-lesbian crew. We had Thursday night, which tends to be the busiest and a big drinking night. There's definitely a very strong and often hostile male presence at the bar. Many of these men didn't know anything about me, about my personal life, but because I was a strong woman, I was automatically labeled a dyke. I think it had a lot to do with being a woman who was in a position of authority and had to enforce the rules about drinking, etc., coming up against a lot of drunk men. I received so much harassment on the job—and death threats on the telephone—and it went on for months. We finally took one man to College Court. It was an exhausting process, but I hope for him an educational one.

Working in the campus bar was not the smartest thing! I really don't know what I was doing there. It can be one of the more unpleasant environments on earth. But I also feel that I made it my own, hiring an all-lesbian crew. We switched to Monday nights and started having some lesbian and gay nights there. It was incredible. We had a great time. People came from neighboring schools in Dutchess County to play with us. There is more awareness now because of the educating that has been going on. The College Regulations Panel has a good understanding of what we mean when we talk about harassment and that has made a huge difference.

I feel very comfortable with myself. For me, even though I had positive experiences with some of the men I was with, there is a wholeness that I feel in being with women. I wouldn't have known I was missing it before, but it has made an incredible difference in my relationships. I hadn't known that being with women was an option. Now that I know, I feel a wonderful calm in my life.

I'm getting my master's degree in English at New York University and have just finished the first draft of my novel. I struggle with finding a balance between writing and activism. I think writing as a lesbian *is* activism, but in terms of time commitments and emotional energy, the work I do as an activist often conflicts with the work I must do as a writer. Both keep me alive; both make me strong. Working out the schedule will be my lifelong ambition.

KIM GLICKMAN

I devoured the article and let myself
feel the huge release of fear and
anger that I had been directing
inward ever since high school. . . .

It was during the second semester of my freshman year at Vassar that I met her. Her name is Jodi. We became friends through a mutual friend who was very dear to both of us. At the time, I was seeing a boy named Dave. I had recently moved out of Strong, the only all-women's dorm on campus, because I felt that I wasn't meeting enough men and moving into a coed dorm would be a way to become more social. Ironically, it was only after I moved into Jewett that I began to seriously question my sexuality.

My relationship with Dave was beginning to follow the same dead-end pattern that all my relationships with men/boys had taken since high school. We would develop a friendship, it would become sexual, and I would call it quits after resigning myself to the sad fact that I was feeling nothing more than superficial comradeship. Most of the time it wasn't even a good friendship. I would stick it out hoping that something would click, until the sexual pressure became too much to bear. I would begin to feel that I was being unfair, leading them to believe I was interested when really I wasn't. The *idea* of a romantic friendship with a man was always far more appealing than the relationship itself. It was painful and frightening to finally acknowledge this to myself and to call the relationships off. By the time Dave and I had reached this point, I was finally

Vassar College Main Building *(photo © Anne MacKay)*

beginning to ask myself some hard questions. Jodi was there to support me through the questioning. Neither of us knew that in the process we would fall in love ourselves.

Jodi was taking Introduction to Women's Studies that semester and was beginning to ask herself questions about sexuality and meet some lesbian feminists on campus. While our group of friends supported her new academic interests, we did not know exactly what to make of her emerging feminist consciousness. For the most part, we were as excited as she was to begin reading and discussing feminist theory. But I remember the sexuality discussions shaking some of us up, myself included, until I began to find comfort in her bold explorations and feel safe to start questioning my own feelings. Dave really wasn't exciting to me, and I soon began to wonder whether men as a class excited me at all. It was terrifying at first, but once I began to ask myself some questions, the answers came pouring out.

I remember Jodi asking me one day in the library if I wanted to read some of the articles she was reading in Women's Studies. She thought they might be interesting to me after I had shared with her some of my fears about loving women. She gave me two articles that day in the library and I will never forget them. The first one was Carroll Smith-Rosenberg's "The Female World of Love and Ritual." It was about 19th century love between women. I had never read anything like it before in my life—an article about the intensity and passion of female friendships, and the ways in which these relationships were primary for them, above and beyond the relationships they had with their husbands. It was truly amazing at 19 years old to be reading a piece of literature that celebrated female/female love rather than denigrated it. I devoured the article and let myself feel the huge release of fear and anger that I had been directing inward ever since high school when I had developed intensely powerful crushes on several of my female teachers. I let the tears pour down my cheeks, feeling relief and joy followed by sadness and anger. Why had I been beating myself over the head all these years? What was I so afraid of? It became very clear to me that female love was beautiful, not ugly, but that it was also intensely threatening to people and because of that I was taught to hate myself for it.

The second article was "Compulsory Heterosexuality and Lesbian Existence," by Adrienne Rich. If the first article wasn't earth-shattering enough for me, this one was truly life-altering. I had indeed been a victim of compulsory heterosexuality. It was as clear to me as day. I did not and had never loved men. I was emotionally, spiritually, and sexually drawn to women. It wasn't until that day in the library that I could let myself know that and actually celebrate it. If I had to pinpoint my coming out to a particular time and place, it would be that afternoon in Lockwood Library of Vassar College. And what a wonderful beginning it was.

Not long after, Jodi and I confessed our love for one another and began to explore the wonders of new lesbian love. Neither of us had been with women before, and so we really found our way together. We were too afraid at that point to tell our group of women friends and so we began sneaking around behind their backs to find time to be alone. We borrowed the room of one of Jodi's lesbian friends (we both had roommates) and would meet there late at night after we parted from our friends. I would go back to Jewett, she to Main, and 15 minutes later we would meet back in this room in Strong. That private space was crucial to us during those last few weeks of the semester. We would retreat to that room sometimes in a panic, other times in a state of exuberance. Our mutual best friend, Michele, was only a few rooms away, and the thought of being found out was somehow both terrifying and thrilling. I was finally discovering a part of myself that was beautiful and alive, passionate and exciting. My own sensuality was so very new to me. I remember feeling as though a part of myself had finally been set free.

It wasn't until the following September that Jodi and I confronted our friends and shared our secret with them. Of course, they had already come to the conclusion themselves over the summer, but it was a huge relief to be able to share our relationship openly with them and find the support we needed.

The lesbian community at Vassar was also integral to my coming out experience. I found the women in the Lesbian Feminist League to be wonderfully supportive, intellectually exciting, and strongly affirming in their attitude toward being a lesbian. It was an important network for me and provided me with a support system as well as some strong role models that I needed to help me build a positive lesbian identity. As I look back on it now, four years later, I feel that there couldn't have been a better time or place for my coming out than during my four years at Vassar.

APPENDIX A

The following letter was written to the
Vassar Alumnae Magazine *in June 1970,*
signed, but with a request for anonymity. It
was returned with the statement: "The
magazine does not accept anonymous
material—either articles or letters."

BEING GAY AT VASSAR

By Anne MacKay '49

—

"Lesbianism is the Achilles' heel of the feminist movement."
—TI-GRACE ATKINSON

"Call them [members of women's liberation] names and they spit on you,
but call them a lesbian and they cry."
—A WOMAN AT A D.O.B. (DAUGHTERS OF BILITIS) MEETING

Because the need for women to relate honestly to other women is increasingly important in the women's movement and because for too long a gentleman's agreement has made lesbianism an undiscussable subject, I hope the editors will allow me to express some views on homosexuality. The prejudice against homosexuals will begin to lift only when lesbians speak the truth for themselves instead of letting ill-informed "experts" or pornographers tell the public.

America treats lesbians as she does blacks: coexistence as long as they don't rock the boat; pretend we're all equal in public but call them queers at home. ("Lesbians are subnatural if they live next door and supernatural if they live in Paris and write books," from *Come Out*, the Gay Liberation Front newspaper.) Even though she must be aware that everyone knows she is a homosexual, it is an act of supreme courage for a woman to come out of the closet and say, "Look at me as I really am. If I am living with someone, recognize that my marriage may be as long-lasting and as affectionate as yours."

When I was at Vassar the silence about homosexuality was immense. No one mentioned some of our best female writers' sexual preferences or acknowledged that some of "Vincent's" love poems were to ladies. Each year there was a new story about roommates who were "too close" and had to be separated, a few giggles about the faculty, but the rest was silence. When I was at Vassar I was not officially gay. (Most women who are not overt homosexuals never dream of labeling themselves gay or lesbian until society forces them to do so.) But I was deeply aware that I was different. I knew that I liked men, wanted them as friends, and could be sexually attracted to them, but my emotional life centered on women.

At that time the textbooks were no help (they're still terrible). Lesbianism was presented as a sickness or perversion or, at best, "arrested development," although doctors did find it odd that homosexuals enjoyed their state so much it was usually impossible to convert them. The best experts now feel that we will never understand homosexuality until we understand the entire process of sexual development, and that research is still lacking.

Most of the work now seems to indicate what homosexuals feel instinctively, that homosexuality is not an illness. For some, it is an imprinting of sexual patterning and identification. Once "set" it is very difficult to change. (For the duckling who was imprinted following a human being instead of a mother duck, it feels *right* to follow human beings and *wrong* to follow ducks. For most lesbians, it feels *right* to love a woman and *wrong* to love a man.) For others, homosexuality may be an accident of time and place and not a confirmed thing at all.

I think there may be many recipes for being homosexual. It is only in the past year, however, that I have become aware of the role society plays in this conditioning. Previously I had looked at my homosexuality only in psychological terms; now I am faced with the Great American Truth: to be a man is to be a person; to be a woman is to be inferior. And woman is always defined in sexual terms; one is only a real woman when one is sexually fulfilled by a man; anything else makes one ersatz, a half-woman.

When I was growing up I never wanted to be a boy or a man or have a penis, but oh, how I wanted the privileges of a man. I was deeply hurt every time my male cousin was taken on the boat and I was not. Boys were expected to achieve something; girls just had jobs. I wanted the freedom to travel on my own without fear of harm or rape. I longed for camaraderie with men or women without sexual hang-ups. But the worst damage was what I did to myself: I accepted and internalized men's view of me. I felt inferior and I was afraid.

To be gay at Vassar was difficult at best: I was surrounded by some of the most attractive people in the world and almost all of them were heterosexual.

To be gay at Vassar was to be very lonely. I know now that Vassar was a terrible and beautiful transition time for many women, but the years seemed especially poignant for me, because I knew I belonged there. I loved the college and the people with a great intensity. My goal (said jokingly) was to climb the water tower and see the entire campus at once. I didn't make it because of those fears, but I knew that the old feminists would have understood such a tomboy action. I did make it up into the cupola of Students' Building* and laughed when I saw the initials there, none carved after the 1920s.

To be gay at Vassar means that you are constantly looking at people (since you're not allowed to ask) to find some clue that another person feels the way you do. You learn painfully that you cannot fall in love with your friends because, of course, they are heterosexual. I did find two people big enough to understand and discuss a little, but no one gave any help. Most people could not even talk about it. I think I understand more now, having seen the very positive reaction most Vassar women had to Lakey, the lesbian in *The Group*. Now, homosexuality is all right to think about, but then, when women were in the process of proving themselves complete by finding men, it was much too threatening.

As a gay person at Vassar I was a flop; I did not find Love

---

*Students' Building is now called the All College Dining Center or ACDC. This gives much amusement to older graduates to whom A/C-D/C meant bisexual.

Students' Building (All College Dining Center) *(photo © Anne MacKay)*

and Happiness. I followed the gentleman's agreement and loved everybody, and they, in return, elected me president of the College Government Association. It was second best, but I was deeply pleased because I felt the affection behind the action.

The young people today are changing the world and I am grateful to them. Their freedom is infectious and has liberated me. They have also freed themselves of the dreadful stereotypes of "You're the boy and I'm the girl." They are neither; they are people, each capable of a range of emotions and behavior. I was very proud when the young Radical Lesbians confronted the Congress to Unite Women in May 1970 and forced them to discuss the homosexual issue. And they did it with humor: banners of "Superdyke Loves You" and "Take A Lesbian to Lunch."

I am not signing this article, even though it may give other CGA presidents heart failure, because my Friend and Longtime Companion (as they say in the obituaries) is not as liberated as I am and the publicity would distress her. I will give my name on request and would be delighted to answer questions.

Appendix B

*The following article is reprinted with
permission from the* Vassar Quarterly,
Winter 1990.

B R E A K I N G   T H E   S I L E N C E :
A Message About Being Homosexual

By Anne MacKay '49

▬

*"Why should I go back to reunion when they don't think I exist, or want
to know about me?"*
—A Vassar alumna from the early 1950s

*"My guess is that there are a large number of lesbian alumnae who
graduated in the days before gay liberation who would welcome a sign of
support from their college....They (like I) probably wonder whether
Vassar has changed any since those days."*
—A Vassar alumna from the late 1960s

Isolation and alienation are recurring themes when gay alumnae/i
exchange memories of Vassar. These feelings have been reinforced
by an impression that homosexuality was a taboo subject, evidenced
by the lack of visibility in the *Vassar Quarterly*—including Class
Notes—and in reunion programs. Until this year, the message from
Vassar seemed clear: homosexuals either did not exist or were beyond the pale and could not be discussed.

Fortunately, the world is changing and Vassar is changing with
it. Subjects once considered unspeakable are now acknowledged. At
my last reunion classmates were talking more freely about their gay
children. President Fergusson has established a standing college
committee to monitor the quality of life for the lesbian and gay
members of the Vassar community, and AAVC has created a struc-

ture to include a lesbian and gay "affinity group." The sad facts are that these actions at Vassar were motivated by reports of discrimination. The following is from an April 1988 proposal for a task force by A Coalition of Concerned Students and Faculty:

> Despite the College's policy of nondiscrimination on the basis of sexual orientation, the continuing instances of harassment reported by gay, lesbian and bisexual students on the campus are alarming. Incidents range from overt threats of physical assault made against gay and lesbian students to more subtle enforcement of anti-gay attitudes in the classroom, where stigma associated with speaking out on gay and lesbian issues often inhibits students from participating fully . . . Gay, lesbian and bisexual employees who wish they could serve as positive role models are reluctant to identify themselves as openly gay for fear of reprisals in the form of harassment from colleagues, or denial of tenure, promotion or renewal of their contracts.

In March of 1990, I and two other gay alumni were asked by the AAVC Ad Hoc Committee to speak to the AAVC Board of Directors and share some of our concerns and experiences. We were pleased to do this, knowing that attitudes change when people get first-hand information and that stereotypes disappear in the face of diversity. Breaking the silence is an important step toward understanding. To this end I also asked the *Quarterly* to run a request for stories about the lesbian and gay experience at Vassar so that I might compile a resource book for students, faculty, and alumnae/i. The replies I have had so far are moving and reflect the difficulty in writing about lives made painful by society, although recent graduates have had an easier time.

When I was at Vassar the silence about homosexuality was immense. The subject simply was not discussed. Faculty never mentioned that many of our best female writers were also lesbian. Even jokes were rarely heard on my corridor. I did hear, long after the fact, that a suicide might have occurred for homosexual reasons, but this was whispered. There was little information on the subject except that one might be "going through a stage" or, possibly, be "an invert," or that all lesbians were very sick. Since the culture said that lesbians were either unattractive and male-identified, or cold, sophisticated, sinister Europeans, who would want to be called a lesbian? Not me! And most women in those days who were emotionally attracted to their own sex would never dream of labeling themselves lesbian. It was a very ugly word.

But for every lesbian there comes a day when two and two add up to something different and one says either "Oh no! That's not me! I'm not some horrible person!" or, "Well, so that's what I am!" Discovering that one is homosexual can come at any time and some women don't find out until late in life. (On a videotape about lesbianism, an extraordinary woman from Boston was interviewed at a gay pride march a few years ago. She said she had had a happy marriage and children, an affair at age 50 that was satisfying, and at age 70 came out as a lesbian.) My day came when I realized that my feelings for women were serious, that sex with men could be nice (or not nice), but was meaningless without the emotional feelings that should accompany it. This moment didn't happen for me until two years after college, and although the realization brought great relief, I still had to deal with the negative messages of society. For some women, finding out they were gay brought terror, hiding, or denial, and often a rush into marriage and children to prove they were "real" women.

If the result was relief and acceptance, the next hurdle was to find someone with whom life could be shared. This, of course, was not so easy when one's applicant pool was a very hidden 10 percent of the female population, of whom some were already married. In my time, the only public places where one met lesbians were gay bars; consequently, alcohol dependence became a major problem for many women. Others would never go into gay bars. I didn't even know they existed. Gay men found bars more easily, but were discouraged from forming couples by a culture which condemned "sissies."

In spite of the problems, one slowly finds friends, and, some years later, instead of being alone one is part of a wonderful group of people, an extended family, a loving community that keeps expanding. Today, lesbian communities exist all over the country.

But being gay in a heterosexual world is far from easy. Discrimination in one's family and profession is discouraging and can be devastating. Street harassment and "gay bashing" are increasing. Children are still removed from lesbians in court cases. Although we know now that child molestation is associated mostly with heterosexual males, homosexuals are still feared as seducers. Even if you saved the general's life in battle, you would still be discharged by the military as "unfit." One alumna from the 1950s writes that in graduate school she fell in love with

> a nice straight girl who turned me into the Dean when the affair got too uncomfortable for her. The Dean sent me to the school shrink who told me I was evil—that's how I heard it— and I was asked to leave school. The Dean, who was very kind, gave me a medical leave. But the event did nothing for my self-esteem. . . . I resolved to be straight and with the help of a lot of alcohol lived a very unhappy heterosexual life for two years. . . . I am still not completely out of the closet because of my job.

Another alumna writes about Vassar in the 1960s:

> I was ostracized by the very people who I thought were my best friends. It seems that if I took up for these lesbian students, I might be one too, and my friends would not accept that possibility. . . . It was a terrible experience and I still feel the pain and bitterness about much of it.

Although I have felt more discrimination as a woman than as a lesbian, I am always aware that people do talk about one's life. Unless one can be open, which is not always easy at work, colleagues do not acknowledge one's lifestyle or partner, and the silence continues. Fortunately, changes in society have allowed many homosexuals to live more freely now. A recent graduate writes:

> Although I am a lesbian now, I thought myself "bi" in my Vassar days. . . . I was extremely comfortable at Vassar . . . the liberal atmosphere I felt at Vassar encouraged me to be "out" after graduation.

The Vassar years for most of us, straight or gay, were wonderful, difficult, or both. Although I did not find "love and happiness" while I was at college, I had the best of times. I loved Vassar and was fortunate to be part of a very special class—'48–49. We had fun together and were always producing shows—we still do, our reunion shows are spectacular! Our early reunions were not so comfortable for me when conversations were centered on husbands and children. But by the time of our 25th reunion things were different. We had survived troubles and illnesses, social status was less important, some husbands had run off, a few had been thrown out for bad behavior, many women were starting new careers, and everyone was talking about things that mattered.

Lesbians and gay men are speaking out whenever they can. Patricia Cain '68 wrote to the AAVC Ad Hoc Committee last year:

I have been open and honest about my lifestyle with all Vassar classmates I have encountered since my years in England. In the early 1970s there was tolerance but discomfort. Today there is much more acceptance. I went to reunion for the first time in June of 1988 and I took my life partner with me. We both had a wonderful time. . . .

. . . As a graduate of Vassar who is in a position to be "out" (I am a tenured law professor), I would like to do what I can to make the Vassar campus safe for the lesbian and gay

Taylor Gate and Vassar College Main Building *(photo by Dixie Sheridan/Courtesy of Vassar College)*

community. Because I am a professor I am in a position to see the problems that plague many college campuses regarding homophobia (and racism and sexism). I have fought hard to keep student gay and lesbian organizations afloat during hard times. . . . If lesbian and gay culture is omitted from the Vassar curriculum, then I believe Vassar is doing its students a grave disservice. At the same time, the silence contributes to the misunderstanding and the prejudice.

I hope that those alumnae/i who are gay and haven't written to me about their experiences at Vassar will try to do so, for while the themes are similar, the stories are all different. Students today who are confronting the need for alternate lifestyles deserve to know about the almost 3,000 graduates who have been there before them.

Appendix C

*Excerpts from a letter written by Pat Cain
'68 to the chairman of the AAVC Ad Hoc
Committee.*

Mr. John B. Wolf
c/o AAVC
Alumnae House
Raymond Avenue
Poughkeepsie, NY 12601

October 27, 1989

RE: Lesbian and Gay Alumnae/i Association

Dear Mr. Wolf:

Thank you for inviting me to comment in writing about the possibility of forming a lesbian and gay alumnae/i association.

In order to explain why I support the idea of a lesbian/gay group within AAVC, I must speak personally about my relationship with Vassar and my present identification as a lesbian. I came to Vassar College in 1963 from Columbus, Georgia, a somewhat narrow-minded small town. In those days, white, middle-class women in Columbus became debutantes, junior leaguers, housewives, and mothers. I felt called by none of those options. Going to Vassar was a form of escape. I had fallen in love with Vassar during my junior year in high school when I visited the campus, attended classes (I remember dissecting *The Waste Land* in Mr. Sherwood's English class), and saw the Drama Department's production of Lillian Hellman's *The Children's Hour*. I was surrounded by smart women who talked about their own ideas, and I had seen a play in which two women were accused of being in love with each other. I had never heard the word lesbian before in my life, and yet I had been in love with women as far back as I could remember. Of course, at the time, I was dating a male high school student. My feelings for women, although emotionally strong, were not sexual. At the time, I would not have called myself a lesbian. But don't think it would have upset me had someone else suggested that I was a lesbian. I'm sure it would have felt absolutely correct.

I know I never thought that loving other women was wrong. And yet I had just seen a play that told me what I knew to be true about most of society—*they* would say it was wrong. The play pushed my "justice button," and my sense was that the Vassar students I was visiting felt the same way. It is no wonder to me, in retrospect, that I considered no school other than Vassar.

My years at Vassar were neither successful, nor particularly happy. I floated from one major to another—physics, philosophy, and finally drama. I had to leave at the end of my second year because my father ran out of money. The school, as a whole, was never supportive of me. But for a few individual souls who did reach out to me, I would have written Vassar off at the time I left. I did return and graduate and I have been minimally supportive of Vassar over the years. I would not be where I am today were it not for Vassar.

I attribute a large part of my failure at Vassar (especially my lack of direction) to the personal turmoil of those years. I never *became* a lesbian at Vassar, although I did try. I discovered that there were students there (one or two anyway) who had a reputation for being lesbian. Although I did not know these students, I found myself automatically taking up for them whenever their "strangeness" was brought up in conversation. The result was that I was ostracized by the very people who I thought were my best friends. It seems that if I took up for these lesbian students, I might be one too, and my friends would not accept that possibility. I quickly found that there was no one to talk to. So I searched for new friends who might listen. And before too long I elected to remain silent, using a journal to keep me sane.

It's hard for me today to believe the sort of strained conversations I had over this issue with classmates who had seemed so open. Vassar, which I had thought of as an escape from small-minded Columbus, Georgia, was being just as small-minded. It was a terrible experience and I still feel pain and bitterness about much of it.

I suspect most of my Vassar friends were unaware of my turmoil. Once the topic was made taboo, my silence enabled us to remain friends. As a result, I still feel some rift between the *true* me and Vassar.

I was unable to find a healthy lesbian community until well after graduation when I was living in London, England. Part of my discomfort over my years at Vassar, especially as to the negative reactions of my peers, was dissipated in London because I had Vassar classmates there who were accepting of my newly chosen lifestyle.

I have been open and honest about my lifestyle with all Vassar classmates I have encountered since my years in England. In the early 1970s there was tolerance but discomfort. Today there is much more acceptance. I went to reunion for the first time in June of 1988 and I took my life partner with me. We both had a wonderful time. There was none of the old ostracism. Indeed, some of the folks I would have pegged as most homophobic were the easiest to be with. The healing of the old Vassar experiences has clearly begun. (And I had a classmate who I had not known in college pull me aside and confess that she had wanted to bring her lesbian partner, but had been afraid to. I encouraged her to bring her to the next reunion.)

There are many reasons I think Vassar needs to do something for lesbian and gay alums. Many of us are "out" in our current lives and many of us are successful at what we do. And I am sure that I am not the only one who looks back at Vassar years with a bit of a cringe. My guess is that there are a large number of lesbian alumnae who graduated in the days before gay liberation who would welcome a sign of support from their college for their chosen lifestyle. They (like I) probably wonder whether Vassar has changed any since those days. I certainly can't tell by reading the *Quarterly*. And the class notes sections are full of marriages, children, and new jobs. Even I have not sent in a card celebrating my lesbian relationship— although, since reunion was so positive, I do intend to do so. (I have run into other lesbians from Vassar who have mused about "coming out" or announcing their relationships in the class notes section. But I don't believe any of them have done so yet.)

Why is the lesbian and gay community at Vassar so invisible? Is it still unsafe at Vassar? I have seen a copy of the 1988 letter to President Fergusson requesting the formation of the task force and the statement of the problem which describes homophobic experiences on the Vassar campus. [This] suggests that it is still unsafe. Establishing a lesbian/gay alumnae/i group is a step toward recognizing lesbian and gay existence. Invisibility means it is not safe to talk and if it is not safe to talk then there is fear and misunderstanding.

As a graduate of Vassar who is in a position to be "out" (I am a tenured law professor), I would like to do what I can to make the Vassar campus safe for the lesbian and gay community. Because I am a professor I am in a position to see the problems that plague many college campuses regarding homophobia (and racism and sexism). I have fought to keep student gay and lesbian organizations afloat during hard times. And I am constantly fighting for more coverage of gay and lesbian issues in the curriculum. I cover the unique legal problems that gay and lesbian clients face in all of my own courses (Income Tax, Wills, and Property), and I have one (straight) colleague who offers similar coverage. If lesbian and gay culture is omitted from the Vassar curriculum, then I believe Vassar is doing its students a grave disservice. At the same time, the silence contributes to the misunderstanding and the prejudice.

Very truly yours,

Patricia A. Cain
Vassar '68